DRAWING
SOMERSET'S PAST

DRAWING SOMERSET'S PAST

An Illustrated Journey Through History
By Time Team Artist Victor Ambrus and Steve Minnitt

Victor Ambrus in association with South West Heritage Trust

Foreword by Sir Tony Robinson

The History Press

First published 2018
Reprinted 2021

The History Press
The Mill, Brimscombe Port
Stroud, Gloucestershire, GL5 2QG
www.thehistorypress.co.uk

© Victor Ambrus, 2018
In Association with South West Heritage Trust
Text by Stephen Minnitt with contributions from Tom Mayberry,
Bob Croft and Sam Astill.

British Library Cataloguing in Publication Data.
A catalogue record for this book is available from the British
Library.

ISBN 978 0 7509 6786 0

Typesetting and origination by The History Press
Printed by Imak, Turkey

CONTENTS

FOREWORD

My abiding memory of Victor Ambrus is at a Channel 4 *Time Team* dig somewhere near Luton overlooking the M1. From the aerial photos we'd scrutinised, we thought we'd probably discovered some kind of ancient structure, but it was only when we started digging that we realised the area was peppered with Roman temples. Our mechanical diggers were working flat-out, our camera teams were criss-crossing hither and thither, our field archaeologists were shifting their spoil heaps from one end of the site to the other, and our specialists were jabbering ten-to-the dozen in a frenzy of excitement. But in the midst of all this orchestrated chaos, sitting on a little canvas chair, was a courteous, smartly dressed, elderly man with a sheaf of pencils and an art pad, totally oblivious to the twenty-first-century distractions which bombarded him, blithely conjuring back to life a vision of the site as it would have been the best part of 2,000 years ago.

I worked with Victor for twenty years, watching him breathe life into the past via its fragile archaeology. His work was always pivotal. He effortlessly provided the colour, human scale and imagination which enabled our viewers to visualise how people lived, worked and died in the past.

This book gathers together a wide range of Victor's paintings, some created for *Time Team*, some special commissions for the Museum of Somerset, and others produced specially for this book. Many are published here for the first time. It has a clear focus on a wide range of archaeological sites from Somerset, but the examples given here are typical of many sites across the whole of Britain.

Looking at the past through the eyes of an artist enables us to appreciate how little we have changed. Victor brings Somerset's past to life from the cave dwellers of Cheddar Gorge through to the festival dwellers of Glastonbury. It is with great pleasure that I invite you to immerse yourselves in our history and prehistory, and enjoy the unique talents of Victor Ambrus.

Sir Tony Robinson, 2018

Sir Tony Robinson. (Photograph by Paul Marc Mitchell)

Time Team in the early days. From left to right, back row: Phil Harding, Geraldine Barber, Victor Ambrus. Front row: Carenza Lewis, Tony Robinson, Mick Aston and Robin Bush.

A reunion of some members of Time Team at the preview of Victor's exhibition 'The Art of Victor Ambrus' at the Museum of Somerset on 22 April 2016: John Gater, Phil Harding, Victor, Tim Taylor (producer) and Stuart Ainsworth.

VICTOR AMBRUS ON SOMERSET

My first experience of Somerset was in my art student days when I was overjoyed to be asked to illustrate several projects for the War Office. This was surprising as I had only recently arrived from the ruins of Budapest following the 1956 Uprising. The train was chugging through the extraordinary Somerset Levels and water was blinking everywhere in the sun. A military vehicle whipped me away from the station (unfortunately, as I could scarcely speak any English at the time, I don't recall the name of it, but it was not so much a station as a military post). I was taken to a huge hangar, in the middle of which were an enormous rocket and a chair for me to sit on.

I soon got cracking on the rocket, which was a new subject to me, with people hovering around me. Eventually, I became conscious of very heavy breathing over my right shoulder – this turned out to be an enormous Alsatian. A jovial military policeman said, 'I would leave off any letters and numbers' and told me to forget them. I never saw those drawings again.

Time Team brought me to Somerset on many occasions. As usual, everything happened suddenly in *Time Team*. Before I knew it, I was on my way to Cheddar Gorge, several hours' journey from where I live. I stood on the balcony of our accommodation and looked down on the dark heart of the gorge and I could not resist doing a small sketch. Some small fires were burning with streaks of smoke reaching up to the sky.

Next day dawned with a lovely morning and Phil was already chipping away on a chunk of flint, Geophiz were arguing over a map and huge bison were beginning to roll off my drawing board. By late afternoon traces of human habitation were discovered – a human bone was found with signs of expert butchering, so I started a drawing showing a group of hunters feasting.

My favourite story was when I was drawing a feast celebrating dead warriors. In order to inherit the warrior's strength and bravery, it was a custom to chew on their bones. A local gentleman asked what I was drawing and when I explained to him, he said, 'People are not going to take kindly to your drawing such a thing.' To which I replied, 'I am sure they have given up such bad habits, and in any case, there is now a superstore around the corner!'

Somerset has produced an amazing variety of sites and subjects – not just the Sweet Track with its peaceful walk but King Alfred's works at Athelney, the Civil War, 'Hanging' Judge Jeffreys' evil doings following the Monmouth Rebellion and more recent events including the Glastonbury Festival. In recent years, I have worked on a wide range of illustrations for the new Museum of Somerset and for the Hinkley Point archaeology project.

I have enjoyed working in Somerset and this book brings together some of my illustrations that tell the story of how people have lived, worked, and shaped this part of England over thousands of years.

Victor at work in the Somerset landscape.
(Photograph by Justin Owen)

Early Times

Hunter-Gatherers: Somerset's Earliest Residents

People first arrived in the area of what is now the county of Somerset some 500,000 years ago. For all but the last 6,000 years, life was sustained by hunting wild animals and gathering plant foods. The earliest humans lived in an environment that included cave bear, rhinoceros, wild dog, jaguar and scimitar-toothed cat amongst the animal population.

Over the past half million years Britain was subject to some of the most rapid and dramatic changes in climate and environment in the history of the earth. For much of the time Somerset was a land of ice and snow. These changes had an enormous impact on people's lives and in particular the wild resources available for food. The changes were so extreme that time and time again people were unable to live in this part of the world; they either moved away or perished. Occasions when human beings were absent could last for a very long time. For example, southern Britain was deserted from 180,000 to 60,000 years ago. The most recent period of depopulation was just 13,000 years ago. There were also warmer periods when hippos lived along riverbanks and wallowed in lakes, and humans seem to have thrived. At such times people lived in the open, perhaps making simple shelters such as tents. In colder periods shelter was sought in caves.

A handaxe in use

Early humans made tools from flint because it was easy to work and could be given a sharp edge. Handaxes provide some of the most important evidence for the presence and activities of early people. Handaxes served a variety of purposes including butchery, working wood and chopping plant materials. They are often described as the equivalent of today's Swiss army knife.

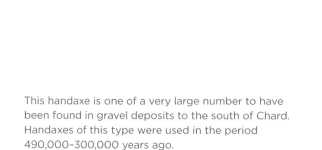

This handaxe is one of a very large number to have been found in gravel deposits to the south of Chard. Handaxes of this type were used in the period 490,000–300,000 years ago.

The Banwell Bear

Many Ice Age animal remains have been found in caves on the Mendip Hills. Over a period of 250,000 years carcasses were washed into these caves by storm water and the bones accumulated. Banwell Bone Cave provides Britain's best evidence of later Ice Age animals. The bison, wolves and reindeer that roamed the frozen Mendip landscape 80,000 years ago are all represented. Most remarkable is the 'Banwell Bear'. The animal stood 2.5m tall and lived predominantly on bison and reindeer.

Banwell Bone Cave was discovered in 1824. The site belonged to the Right Reverend George Law, Bishop of Bath and Wells. Law employed local farmer William Beard over many years to undertake the excavation and collection of many thousands of animal bones that lay buried within the cave. The skull of the Banwell Bear is one of Beard's most important discoveries.

Bishop Law believed that the bones were evidence for the Great Flood described in the Book of Genesis in the Bible, and opened the Bone Cave to the public. At the entrance to the cave were the following words:

Here let the scoffer of God's holy word
Behold the traces of the deluged world,
Here let him behold in Banwell Cave t'adore
The Lord of Heaven, then go and scoff no more.

Hunters in the Hyena Den,
Wookey Hole

After a long period of absence people returned to the area about 60,000 years ago. These were humans of Neanderthal type. They were few in number and lived in small groups. Caves in Somerset have produced evidence of occupation at this time, including the Hyena Den, a small cave at Wookey Hole on the Mendip Hills where people lived about 45,000 years ago. The Hyena Den was discovered accidentally in 1852 by workmen cutting a new leat for a paper mill. Since then it has undergone a series of excavations. The site lay at the end of a ravine and would have been an ideal location for a hunting camp and for trapping game. Animal species represented by bones found in the Hyena Den included spotted hyena, woolly rhinoceros and wild horse. The site produced flint tools and some of the earliest evidence for the use of fire in Somerset.

Hunting a woolly mammoth

Grazing mammoths helped to keep the landscape clear during colder periods. They closely cropped the plants and grasses, and prevented trees from growing. An adult male mammoth could weigh more than 6 tonnes and stand 4.3m at the shoulder. Woolly mammoths had small ears, a sloping back, a long woolly coat and large tusks. One animal would have provided a considerable amount of meat for a hunting group. Their skin, bones and tusks would all have been put to good use. Woolly mammoths may have survived in southern Britain until 12,000 years ago. Hunting contributed to their extinction but climate change and the encroachment of trees into the landscape with a consequent reduction in their favoured habitat was also a cause.

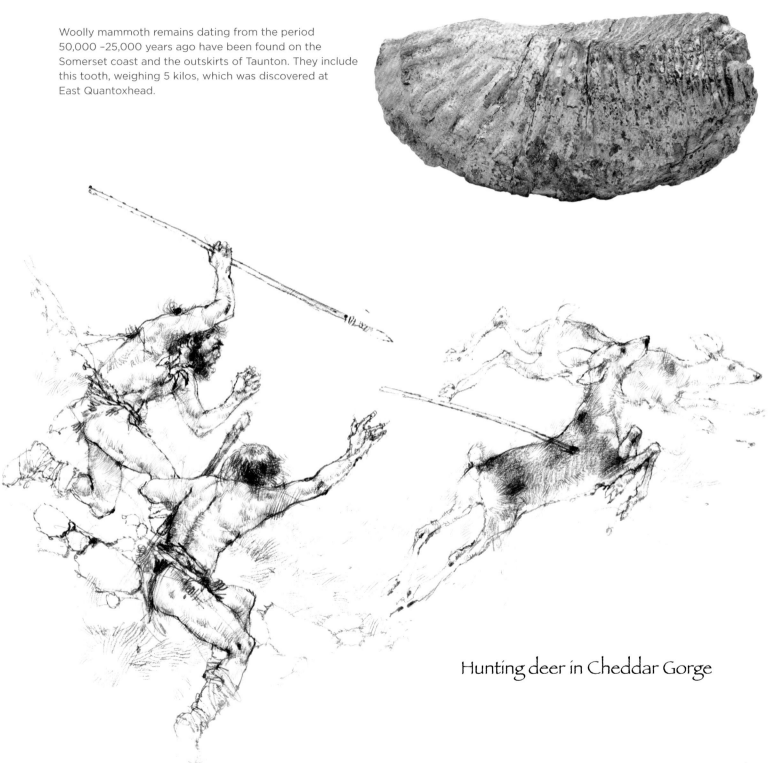

Woolly mammoth remains dating from the period 50,000 –25,000 years ago have been found on the Somerset coast and the outskirts of Taunton. They include this tooth, weighing 5 kilos, which was discovered at East Quantoxhead.

Hunting deer in Cheddar Gorge

A hunter in Cheddar Gorge

Gough's Cave, on the southern side of Cheddar Gorge, is the richest site in Britain for finds of flint tool from the later part of the Palaeolithic. As with many important archaeological sites, it was discovered accidentally. The caves in Cheddar Gorge were a popular tourist destination in the later 1800s. In 1890 local man Richard Gough decided to try and benefit from this and started to open up the mouth of a cave which until then had only been a minor visitor attraction. In the process of improving access Gough discovered considerable quantities of flint and animal bone. The tools included knives, the tips of spears, scrapers for preparing animal skins and awls for piercing the skins. Subsequent work has shown that flint used to make the tools probably came from the area of Salisbury Plain, about 70km away, indicating that people moved over wide areas or that there was a system of exchange.

Animal bones found at Gough's Cave paint a vivid picture of Somerset about 14,700 years ago, near the end of the last Ice Age. There were large herbivores such as red deer and giant ox, smaller mammals like badger, wolf and arctic hare, and birds including black grouse and partridge. Large herds of wild horse were the main source of meat for people living in Gough's Cave. Cut marks on the animal bones show that the carcases were skinned and butchered carefully.

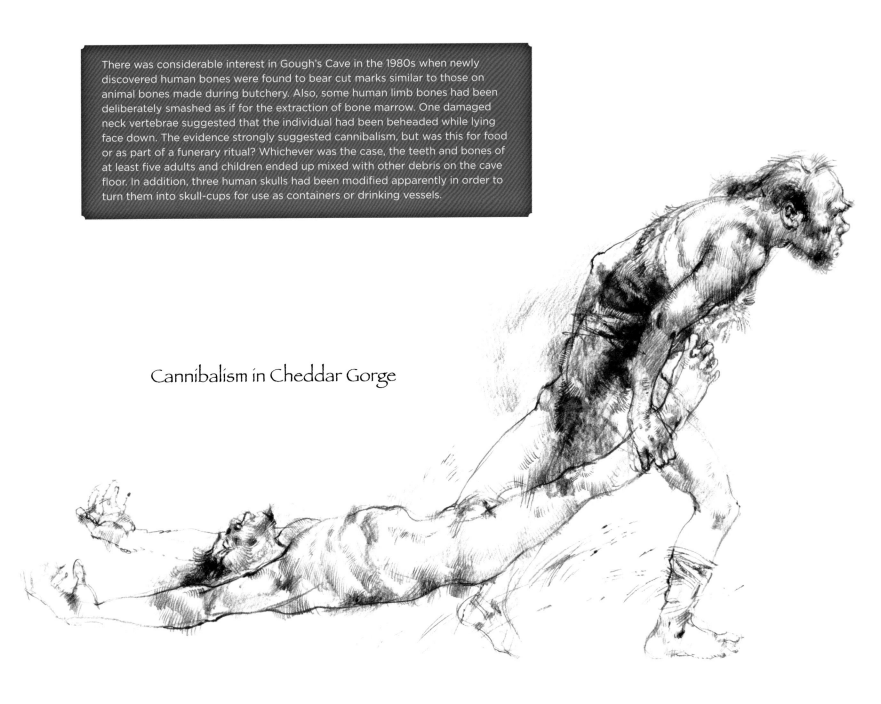

There was considerable interest in Gough's Cave in the 1980s when newly discovered human bones were found to bear cut marks similar to those on animal bones made during butchery. Also, some human limb bones had been deliberately smashed as if for the extraction of bone marrow. One damaged neck vertebrae suggested that the individual had been beheaded while lying face down. The evidence strongly suggested cannibalism, but was this for food or as part of a funerary ritual? Whichever was the case, the teeth and bones of at least five adults and children ended up mixed with other debris on the cave floor. In addition, three human skulls had been modified apparently in order to turn them into skull-cups for use as containers or drinking vessels.

Cannibalism in Cheddar Gorge

Hunter-gatherers on the shore of the Severn Estuary

About 10,000 years ago the final cold phase of the Ice Age came to an abrupt end, perhaps over a period of only fifty years. As a result of the rise in temperature southern England was colonised first by birch woodland, then forests of hazel, pine and oak. This changed environment provided new and varied food resources. Animal populations included red deer, roe deer, aurochs (wild ox) and pig. There were abundant fish, shellfish and waterfowl in the rivers, lakes and sea. Nuts, berries, edible roots and plants were available according to the seasons of the year. People once again lived in the open rather than sheltering from the cold in caves. They probably moved around according to season to take advantage of food resources and over the years returned to the same campsites many times.

Recent DNA analysis on a male skeleton found over a century ago in Gough's Cave, Cheddar, has provided an insight into the appearance of people 10,000 years ago. He had dark skin, brown curly hair and blue eyes.

New types of flint tools were developed. Axes with wooden handles were made and small blades known as microliths were used as tips and barbs for arrows. Surface scatters of flints reveal where people lived. The locations range from islands in the Somerset wetlands to high up on the hills of Exmoor.

One consequence of the rise in temperature was the release of enormous amounts of water as the vast tracts of ice further north melted. The resulting dramatic rise in sea level created new landscapes including the Severn Estuary. Tree stumps and roots can still be seen at some coastal locations in west Somerset, a relic of a time when the sea level was lower and the area was forested. The wild aurochs is the ancestor of today's cattle. Wild aurochs first appeared in Britain 400,000 years ago and are associated with warm climates and mixed or deciduous woodland. They lived in boggy areas on the edge of forests and ate grasses, leaves and bark. The bulls were large in size with horns that could do an enormous amount of damage to a human. In spite of the challenge they presented to hunters, aurochs were a favoured source of meat in the Mesolithic period. Aurochs remains have been found at various locations in Somerset including Sutton Bingham, Bridgwater, Dulcote and Greylake, Middlezoy. Wild aurochs were eventually hunted to extinction in Britain during the Bronze Age.

Hunting an aurochs 9,000 years ago

The Sweet Track

Somerset's first farmers

The introduction of farming to Britain about 6,000 years ago was to have a dramatic impact on human lifestyle. People no longer needed to follow their food resources according to the seasons of the year. Farming tied communities to the land in new ways. A new annual cycle was created based upon planting, harvesting and storing crops. Crops had to be protected from wild animals and domestic animals had to be prevented from straying. Farming enabled people to live in more permanent settlements. This new way of life required new tools. They included polished stone axe heads that were used to clear land of trees ready for farming and flint tools that met the needs of the changed lifestyle. Pottery, which was used for cooking and storage, was also introduced at this time. Of all the human activities that have affected our landscape in prehistoric and historic times, agriculture has had the greatest impact.

Wood was a very important raw material in the later prehistoric period. It was used in the construction of houses and in the making of tools and equipment. However, structures and objects of wood rarely survive. Somerset is exceptional for the quantity of worked prehistoric wood that has been preserved in the waterlogged peat of the central part of the county. Wooden trackways, which enabled movement across the marshes, have survived in a remarkably good state of preservation. These trackways were made in different ways in response to different environments. In areas of shallow water raised walkways were sometimes constructed, whilst on the wet surfaces of raised bogs wattlework panels or simple deposits of brushwood met their needs. Amongst these trackways is the Sweet Track, a 2km-long walkway of raised planks that enabled people to cross a reed swamp. The Sweet Track ran north from the Polden Hills to the island of Westhay. It is one of the most complex trackways yet discovered and demonstrates the woodworking skills and organisation of those involved in its creation. The tools used comprised polished stone axes and mallets and wedges made from wood. Some of the oak trees felled to make the planks for the walkway were up to 1m in diameter. Tree-ring dating shows that the Sweet Track was constructed during the winter of 3807/06 BC. In spite of the effort required to build and maintain this trackway it was only used for about ten years. A number of objects, including pottery and a very fine jadeite axe, were placed beside the trackway, probably as offerings.

Science can help to unlock the secrets of ancient objects. Amongst the objects found beside the Sweet Track was this bowl. The clay of the bowl has been analysed and was found to contain traces of fat which show that it held milk products, probably butter. This provides some of the earliest evidence for dairying in Britain.

An early farming community at Shapwick

Surface scatters of flint and stone tools and occasional sherds of pottery found in ploughed fields are the main indications for the location of settlement sites of the first farmers in Somerset. These finds help to shed light on the activities that took place. Flint flakes and cores provide evidence for flint knapping and the production of tools, axes show woodworking, flint tools such as scrapers and awls suggest the working of leather or animal skins or food preparation, whilst arrowheads represent hunting or warfare. Pottery was used for the preparation and storage of food. This drawing shows a small community of farmers in the parish of Shapwick about 5,000 years ago.

Wick Barrow, in the parish of Stogursey, is a rare example of a Neolithic round barrow, dating from about 5,600 years ago. The mound measures about 25m in diameter and 1.5m in height. Archaeologists discovered the partial remains of five adults and one child within a 10m-diameter drystone walled enclosure that was covered by a mound of earth.

About 4,500 years ago, small groups of settlers arrived in Britain bringing with them a way of life that included new burial rites, the first use of metal (copper and gold) and distinctive forms of pottery known today as Beakers. Their way of dealing with the dead focused on the individual concerned and contrasted with the practice of communal burial then in vogue in Britain. These incomers seem initially to have lived separately from the indigenous population. Rather than construct a new round barrow for burials, a local group of 'Beaker People' made use of Wick Barrow. Three adult males were buried in the mound about 4,400 years ago. Each was placed separately in a crouched position on their side and was accompanied by a Beaker. We can imagine that the funeral ceremonies would have been quite elaborate as these men would have been important figures in society.

Wick Barrow was excavated in 1907 by Harold St George Gray of the Somerset Archaeological and Natural History Society. The excavation was sponsored by the Viking Society in the belief that it could be a Viking burial. The circular drystone wall constructed to house the earliest burials can be clearly seen. (Photograph courtesy of Somerset Archaeological and Natural History Society)

Victor on the site of Wick Barrow sketching in preparation for his drawing of the burial procession. Wick Barrow burial mound can be seen in the background. (Photograph by Justin Owen)

These finely decorated earthenware Beakers were placed with burials in Wick Barrow. Research on Beakers found elsewhere has shown that some of these vessels may have contained an alcoholic, honeyed drink similar to mead. A recent study of the DNA of the burial associated with the Beaker on the right, a young male aged around 20 years, has revealed that he came from the area of what is now the Netherlands. More than that, he almost certainly had brown eyes and red hair.

Wick Barrow is also known as Pixie's Mound, a name derived from local folklore. According to legend, a ploughman working nearby heard what he believed to be the sound of a small child crying, coming from bushes on the mound. Unbeknown to the ploughman it was actually the voice of a pixie! The pixie was complaining that he had broken his peel – a flat wooden shovel used for putting loaves of bread into baking ovens. When the ploughman went to investigate, he found a tiny wooden peel with its handle broken. Still thinking that it was a child who would eventually return for their toy, he mended the peel and left it where he had found it. When his day's work was over, the ploughman went to see if the toy had been taken. It was gone, but in its place he found a reward, a beautiful cake hot from the pixie's oven. Prehistoric round barrows and stone circles often have folklore associated with them. The stories provided an explanation for these sites at a time when their dates, creators and purposes were a mystery.

A Wick Barrow pixie!

The Bronze Age

Metalworking technology reached Britain in about 2500 BC. Initially only copper and gold were used, but the former was soon being alloyed with tin to produce the much more effective and useful bronze. New kinds of tools, weapons and personal ornaments were created. Metal objects are often found in hoards. Some hoards may have been hidden for safety or were intended for recycling but most were probably offerings to the gods. Weaponry, including daggers, rapiers, swords and shields, shows that warriors had become important figures in society.

People continued to have a growing impact on the landscape, including its division into fields. This period also provides the earliest clear evidence for houses in Somerset. Roundhouses made from stone and timber have, for example, been found at Brean Down. The excavations at Brean Down also produced the earliest evidence in Somerset for the extraction of salt from seawater.

Round barrows are the most common survival from the Bronze Age in the Somerset landscape. Nearly 600 barrows are known in the county. They are largely to be found on the higher lands of Exmoor and the Quantock and Mendip Hills. Sometimes they occur singly and sometimes in groups. This aerial photograph shows the Ashen Hill barrow group at Priddy. Usually a barrow was built over the remains of a single individual, who was often placed in a pit or stone-lined cist. Other burials were frequently added to the mound. Inhumation was practised initially but was later replaced by cremation with the ashes often being placed in a pottery urn.

This hoard of Bronze Age metalwork was discovered in peat at Edington Burtle in 1854. The hoard comprises sickles, palstaves (axes), bracelets and rings. The bronzes, which date from 1400–1200 BC, were found inside a small wooden box that disintegrated shortly after discovery.

The South Cadbury shield

During excavations at South Cadbury in 1997 a remarkable discovery was made. A sheet bronze shield was found in the upper fill of a Bronze Age ditch. The South Cadbury shield is one of only twenty or so similar shields to have been found in Britain. It is 60cm in diameter and is decorated with twenty-five rows of raised ribs and twenty-five rows of small bosses. There were about 6,030 bosses, each individually stamped. The metal of the shield is only about 1mm in thickness, leading to the belief that it was an object used for display and prestige rather than for the protection of a warrior in combat.

The South Cadbury shield was made in the period 1350–1150 BC. In about 1000 BC it was laid front face down in its final resting place in the ditch and was stabbed three times. This was probably a ritual act of destruction.

The South Cadbury shield was at least 150 years old when it was placed in the ditch and irreparably damaged. The age of the shield at the time of its deposition shows it to have been a valued and treasured object over several generations. Its destruction represented a very significant sacrifice. The three dark areas in the photograph show the points at which the shield was stabbed through.

Ritual activity at Greylake, Middlezoy

Time Team carried out an excavation at Greylake, Middlezoy, in 1998. The excavation provided evidence for the treatment of the dead about 3,000 years ago in the later Bronze Age. Human bones were found together with sheep jaw bones, pottery and a bronze axe that had been intentionally damaged. They lay in what was then an area of shallow water with patches of reeds and fen woodland. The finds were associated with a timber structure that included a series of oak posts. Indications are that the body, or bodies, had been de-fleshed by exposure before being deposited in the water

The Iron Age

About 2,700 years ago iron began to replace bronze as the preferred raw material for making tools and weapons. Working with iron required new skills and the blacksmith became an important person in society. Tribal territories became defined during the Iron Age. Somerset lay within the areas of three tribes – the Dobunni in north-east Somerset and Gloucestershire, the Durotriges in south-east Somerset and Dorset and the Dumnonii of west Somerset, Devon and Cornwall.

The most visible traces of the Iron Age in the Somerset landscape are hillforts. They served as places of defence and symbols of power and authority, but they were also centres of trade, craft and industry. Even today many of these hillforts can be recognised as remarkable feats of construction. Amongst them is Ham Hill which, with a defended area of 88 hectares, is possibly the largest hillfort in the country.

Cadbury Castle in south-east Somerset is a medium-sized hillfort, one of several thousand in Britain. It has very imposing ramparts and a present-day status enhanced by its association with the legendary figure of King Arthur. Hillforts seem to have been built in a relatively short space of time, perhaps over just two or three years, but were then frequently rebuilt or modified. There must have been a large and highly organised labour force available at such times. The first defensive bank and ditch at Cadbury Castle was built in about 400 BC and had a circuit of over 1km. By around 300 BC the defences had been dramatically upgraded to four concentric rings of banks and ditches, an enormous undertaking which required careful planning and organisation. Within the hillfort most of the population lived close to the ramparts, which would have provided some protection from bad weather in this very exposed location. Grain harvested from the land around the hillfort was stored in pits. There is evidence for craft, industry and trade. There is also evidence for ritual including the careful placing of ox skulls in pits and the burial of axes, knives and reaping tools.

Cadbury Castle hillfort from the air. The ramparts which surround the hilltop are mostly covered by trees but they are visible towards the right in this photograph.

Cadbury Castle hillfort

Glastonbury Lake Village

Glastonbury Lake Village in central Somerset is the best-preserved Iron Age settlement in Britain. The settlement was constructed on an artificial island of timber, stone and clay which lay in an environment of open water, reeds and fenwood. From small beginnings in about 200 BC it grew to become a settlement of about fifteen roundhouses and 200 people. The houses had walls of vertical posts in-filled with wattle and daub. The roofs were thatched and the floors were made from clay. Everything, including the enormous quantities of material needed to create the island and build the houses, had to be transported in by canoe. On the eastern side of the settlement was a landing stage for water traffic. The buildings, other structures and the finds provide an unparalleled insight into the industrial, domestic and personal life of an Iron Age community. Glastonbury Lake Village was deserted by about 50 BC, probably due to difficulties caused by rising water levels.

While we have few clues about furniture, decoration or how daily life was organised inside a roundhouse, we can be sure that people would have made things as comfortable as possible.

Interior of an Iron Age roundhouse

Glastonbury Lake Village was discovered by Arthur Bulleid, a young man from Glastonbury. Bulleid developed an interest in the Neolithic Swiss lake villages and became convinced that the wetlands in the vicinity of Glastonbury could contain something similar. In 1892, after four years of searching, he noticed some low mounds in a field. On investigation Bulleid discovered pottery and animal bone in molehills in the field. He got permission from the farmer to carry out a small excavation and quickly realised that he had discovered the type of settlement that he was searching for. With the support of the Glastonbury Antiquarian Society, Bulleid undertook a programme of excavation on the site that ran from 1892 to 1898 and 1902 to 1907. (Photograph courtesy of Somerset Archaeological and Natural History Society)

Canoes were an important form of transport during the Iron Age. They were used to carry people, goods and animals. This canoe, made from the trunk of a large oak tree, was discovered in peat at Shapwick in 1906. It is 6m in length and dates from about 350 BC.

There is a long history of artists creating archaeological and historical scenes in order to bring the past alive. Because of the remarkable preservation of the evidence several artists have produced work based on the site of Glastonbury Lake Village. This view of the settlement is one of a series by Amedée Forestier that was commissioned by the *Illustrated London News* in 1911.

An Iron Age settlement at Stogursey

Most people lived on dry land in the Iron Age and the Somerset landscape was dotted with farmsteads and small settlements with surrounding fields. Farming sustained life. This drawing shows one of few such sites to have been excavated in the county. It was home to a small community in Stogursey parish in about 500 BC. The excavation was part of the programme of fieldwork carried out in advance of the construction of Hinkley Point C power station.

Victor in his studio working on the drawing of the Iron Age settlement at Stogursey. (Photograph by Justin Owen)

ROMAN SOMERSET

The Romans began their invasion of Britain in AD 43. The invading army comprised four legions together with cavalry and auxiliaries, a total of about 40,000 men. Two of the tribes that inhabited Somerset, the Durotriges in the south and the Dumnonii in the west, seem to have been hostile to the newcomers. Their resistance was in vain and Somerset soon became part of the Empire. The conquest and consolidation of southern Britain, including the South West, was carried out by the Second Legion Augusta under the command of future emperor Vespasian.

To begin with, life for many people probably continued largely unchanged. However, as time went on the impact of the Roman way of life increased with the creation of towns such as those at Ilchester and Shepton Mallet, the construction of a network of roads, villas at the centres of wealthy farming estates, the establishment of new industries and access to a range of goods imported from the Continent, including pottery and wine.

By AD 47 Somerset was under Roman control, though the memories of many were probably still raw. Forts were built at a number of locations including Ilchester and Ham Hill to house soldiers whose role was to maintain control and keep the peace. As the frontier extended and life became more stable there was no need for a significant military presence and the forts in the area were abandoned. The civilian settlement that had grown up around the fort at Ilchester remained and became a town.

Soldiers of the Second Legion Augusta shortly after their arrival in Somerset

Lead working at Charterhouse on Mendip

The Romans quickly took control of Somerset's mineral resources including lead on the Mendip Hills. Lead extraction was initially under imperial control and a detachment of soldiers was based at Charterhouse on Mendip to oversee the work. The soldiers came from the Second Legion Augusta. In the second century AD the industry was transferred into private ownership. A large town grew up at Charterhouse as a result of the lead working industry. The sites of buildings and the lines of streets can still be seen today as earthworks in the landscape.

Lead from the Mendips was exported to many parts of the empire. It was also used locally to make water pipes and coffins and was mixed with tin from Cornwall to make pewter. Lead smelting took place on an industrial scale. The processes would undoubtedly have been detrimental to the health of those involved. Even today there are areas where the soil is contaminated with Roman toxic waste.

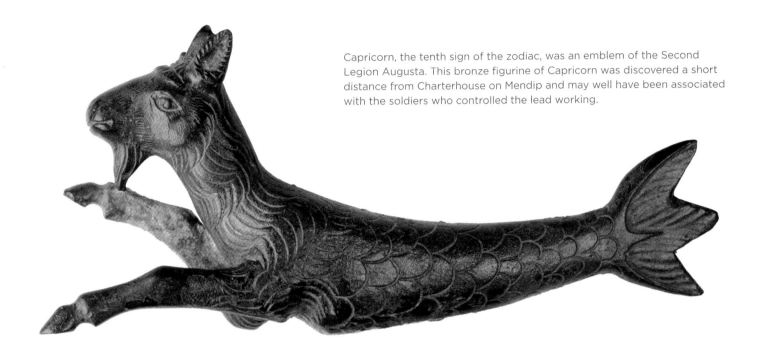

Capricorn, the tenth sign of the zodiac, was an emblem of the Second Legion Augusta. This bronze figurine of Capricorn was discovered a short distance from Charterhouse on Mendip and may well have been associated with the soldiers who controlled the lead working.

Once smelted, the lead was cast into blocks known today as pigs. When lead working was under imperial control lead pigs carried inscriptions bearing the name of the reigning emperor. This pig was found at Chewton Mendip and carries the name of emperor Vespasian, who ruled the Roman Empire from AD 69 to 79.

Burial of a child at Shapwick

Extensive archaeological fieldwork in the parish of Shapwick has revealed much about life and death in the Roman period. There were perhaps four villas, a large agricultural settlement and a landscape dotted with farmsteads. While adults were buried outside settlements, infants were often buried within them. A number of burials of newborn babies were found during excavations on sites at Shapwick. One was found beneath the floor of a high-status fourth-century building. The baby was placed with the skull of a young sheep and five hind feet from three different sheep. The significance of this is uncertain, but they could have been the remains of a meal that formed part of the burial ceremony.

Somerset has become renowned for the number of Roman coin hoards found in the county. Amongst them are some exceptionally large and important hoards. In 1998 a hoard of 9,238 silver denarii was found at Shapwick. It is by far the largest hoard of denarii ever found in Britain. Subsequent geophysical survey and excavations showed that the hoard had been buried under the floor of a small room in a previously unknown Roman villa. The villa was of courtyard type and over time underwent a number of modifications. The drawing shows the villa in its final phase with three ranges set around a courtyard. The incremental development of the villa is reflected in different building styles. The courtyard could well have been an ornamental garden with lawns and pathways. There could also have been paddocks, kitchen gardens, orchards and perhaps even a vineyard. The discovery of bones of duck, teal and corncrake indicate wildfowling in the nearby wetlands. In spite of the apparent wealth of the owner, indicated not least by the coin hoard, the villa appears never to have had the usual luxury features of mosaic floors, plastered and painted walls or an underfloor central heating system.

The Shapwick Roman villa

The Shapwick hoard of silver denarii was buried around AD 225 and represents a large sum of money, the equivalent of perhaps a quarter of a million pounds in today's terms. We don't know why the coins were hidden and never spent. The villa seems to have been demolished shortly after the hoard was buried, perhaps because of a major fire.

The Frome coin hoard

In 2010 Dave Crisp discovered a coin hoard in a field near Frome. The hoard consisted of a large earthenware pot containing 52,503 coins and is the largest hoard of Roman coins ever found in a single container in Britain. Five of the coins are silver; the others are all copper alloy. The hoard was buried in about AD 290, a time when Britain had broken away from the Roman Empire and was under the control of the usurper Carausius.

The Frome hoard called into question the usual assumption that most coin hoards were buried for reasons of security and that when not retrieved and spent were presumed to represent someone's misfortune. Study of the coins in the Frome hoard showed that they had been added to the pot in batches, perhaps tipped in from bags or smaller pots. The coins weighed about 160kg in total. It would have been impossible to lift the pot and coins

from the ground. The only way of retrieving the coins would have been to remove them in handfuls. As a consequence of this, and the fact that it was buried close to a spring, it is believed that the hoard was a votive offering and that it was never intended to be recovered. This raises the question of how many other Roman coin hoards were also offerings?

On 11 April 2010 Dave Crisp received an unusual response from his metal detector and decided to investigate. He dug down to a depth of about 30cm at which point he came across some bronze coins which were clearly part of a hoard. Dave did the correct thing and reported his discovery to the Portable Antiquities Scheme so that it could be investigated archaeologically. As a consequence, much has been learned about the hoard and its deposition that would have been lost had it simply been lifted from the ground by the finder. (Photographs by Pauline Rook)

Life for Roman landowners was often very comfortable. The wealthiest people lived in fine villas with bath suites, central heating and highly decorated rooms. They were centres of family life and business activity. Somerset villas and town houses belonging to the more affluent often had mosaic floors. Most mosaics are patterned but others feature representations of gods and goddesses or animals. The villa at Pitney was discovered in 1828–29, following which it was extensively excavated. It consisted of a series of buildings around a rectangular courtyard. The main living rooms included one of Somerset's finest mosaics with Bacchus, the god of wine, at its centre. This drawing shows the villa in about AD 350 with members of the owner's family, workers and slaves. It would have been a hive of activity.

Pitney Roman villa

A villa at Lopen is one of a number to have been identified in Somerset in recent years. The chance discovery in 2001 of one of the villa's mosaics was down to the sharp eyes of digger driver George Caton, who was undertaking work at Mill House Farm in Lopen. Excavations revealed a mosaic of exceptional size. Archaeologist Alan Graham is shown carefully excavating the area of the mosaic that features a dolphin. There were a number of areas of damage to the mosaic, including one visible in the centre of this photograph. The damage probably occurred in the fifth century when Britain was no longer part of the Roman Empire and life for all was very different. Owners often appear to have abandoned parts of their villas or to have turned them over to other uses such as workrooms or stores.

Mosaic floors were created by laying tesserae, small cubes of stone or tile, in wet lime mortar. Tesserae were made using a hammer and anvil or iron pliers. They were usually made from raw materials derived from local sources. Somerset tesserae are frequently made from blue and white lias and orange-coloured tile. Generally speaking, the smaller the tesserae, the finer the mosaic.

Making tesserae

Laying the Lopen mosaic

The Lopen mosaic measures 12m by 6.8m and is one of the largest mosaic floors to have been found in Britain. It is estimated that around one million tesserae would have been required to create the mosaic. It lay within a substantial Roman villa. The mosaic is patterned but includes a number of motifs such as stylised flowers, drinking cups, a fish and a lively looking dolphin.

The Roman villa at Dinnington was first noticed on aerial photographs taken during the drought of 1976. The villa lay just off the Fosse Way 15km south-west of the Roman town of Ilchester. It is one of about fifty villas that clustered around Ilchester.

Excavations took place at Dinnington between 2002 and 2007. On two occasions the work formed part of Channel 4's *Time Team* series. Other excavations took place as part of a project jointly run by Somerset County Council and the University of Winchester. Dinnington proved to be a particularly large villa with buildings around three sides of a courtyard and a possible gateway and wall on the fourth side. The villa had the usual features of mosaics, painted wall plaster, hypocausts and bathing facilities. Dinnington villa was at its height of prosperity during the fourth century. However, circumstances changed dramatically towards the end of the century when the luxurious west wing was converted for use as grain storage, grain drying and metalworking. The conversion work involved serious damage to mosaics. The villa seems to have become more of a working farm than a place of fine living. The villa continued in use in this way into the fifth century and perhaps even as late as the sixth century.

Dinnington Roman villa

Victor at work at Dinnington during a *Time Team* shoot. (Photograph by Pauline Rook)

Although most of the mosaics at Dinnington were seriously damaged, some clearly included figures in their design. These fragments are from the floor of what was probably a luxurious winter dining room. They depict the water nymph Daphne being transformed into a laurel bush as she attempts to escape the amorous attentions of Apollo, a story told by Ovid in his *Metamorphoses*.

The excavation at Dinnington was part of Time Team's 2005 'Big Roman Dig'. Phil Harding at work is being watched by Professor Tony King, Bob Croft, Victor Ambrus, Councillor Justin Robinson and Mick Aston.

A river mooring south of Hinkley Point

A large number of archaeological sites were discovered in 2012–15, prior to work beginning on the construction of Hinkley Point C. One of the most extensive sites was on the north side of a small stream that flowed towards Wick Moor on the east side of Hinkley Point.

Evidence for Iron Age and Roman occupation was recorded here including farm buildings, yards and fields. It is clear from the pottery evidence that occupation continued in this area for several hundred years, well into the fourth century AD. It is thought that this stream-side settlement would have had good access to the sea by using small boats to take goods in and out, thereby linking this farm to the Severn Estuary and beyond. Fishing net weights, a possible anchor stone and extensive deposits of shellfish were recovered from the site.

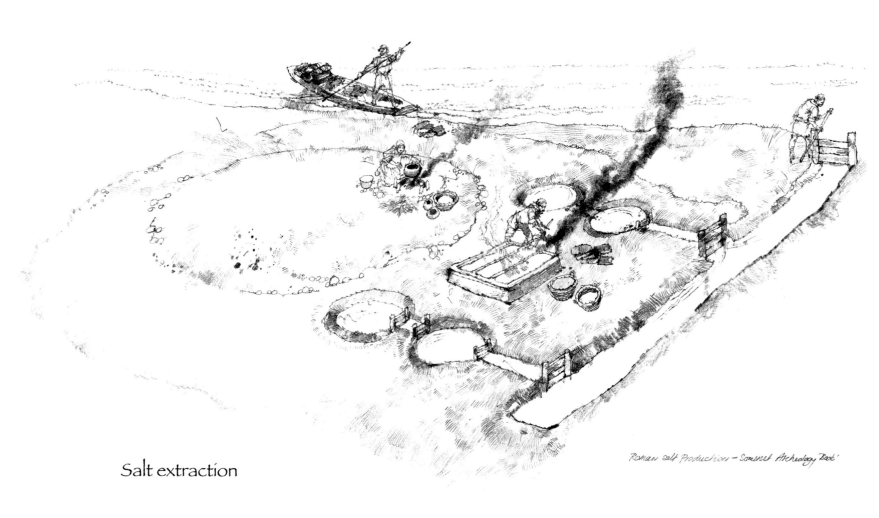

Roman salt Production – Somerset Archeology Dept

Salt extraction

Salt was an important commodity for preserving perishable food and for use as seasoning. Salt production was a significant industry in the Huntspill area in the Roman period. Seawater was collected in shallow ponds or reservoirs and the sediments allowed to settle. The water was transferred to clay pans where it was boiled. The water evaporated, leaving the salt. Sites where salt production took place can be identified by accumulations of fragments of the clay water boiling vessels and quantities of charcoal. Whilst some salt would have been used locally, the scale of salt extraction in this area suggests that it was also being traded further afield.

Lamyatt Beacon Romano-
British temple

Prominent hilltops were favoured sites for temples in the later Roman period. One such site is Lamyatt Beacon near Bruton. Temples such as this were shrines or sanctuaries presided over by priests. People went there to make requests and to give offerings. They were not places for group worship. The central two-storey building was the main shrine or home of the deity and probably held a cult statue. Lamyatt Beacon temple may have been dedicated to Mars. Around the main shrine was a roofed corridor which probably contained altars, statues and places for offerings. Two more smaller shrines flanked the entrance. They may have been dedicated to other gods. Excavations produced many hundreds of coins, items of jewellery and miniature pots. They represent some of the offerings made at the temple.

The Romans believed in many gods and sought their help with everyday problems. These figurines were found in the Roman temple at Lamyatt Beacon. They represent Hercules (god of victory), Minerva (goddess of wisdom and healing), Mars (god of war) and Mercury (messenger of the gods). Christianity became the official Roman religion in AD 313 but many people still worshipped the old gods.

ARTHUR TO ALFRED

The Romans left Britain in about AD 410. We know very little about Somerset in the following 300 years. Gradually Anglo-Saxon newcomers took control of the area and by 845 they had created a 'shire' called Somerset, part of the Anglo-Saxon kingdom of Wessex. The shire covered an area from the River Avon in the north to Exmoor in the west. That landscape had already been shaped by human activity over countless centuries. The archaeological evidence for the period before the tenth century is very limited as a lack of diagnostic artefacts makes sites hard to recognise. The landscape comprised large estates belonging to the king, nobles and, increasingly, the Church. Many of Somerset's towns were established at this time including Frome, Bruton, Langport, Milborne Port, Taunton and Watchet.

Arthur's army

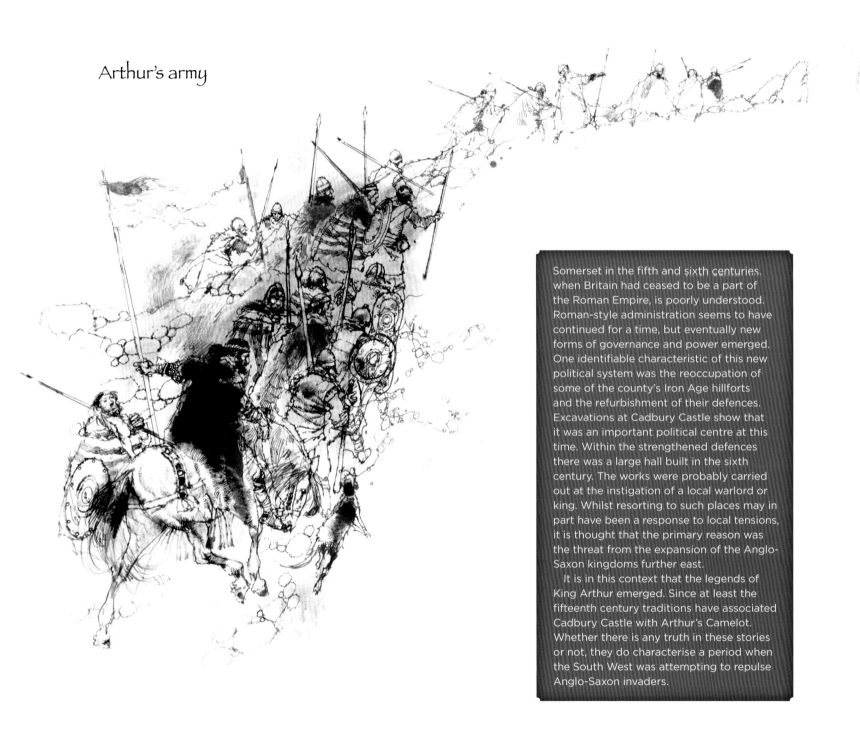

Somerset in the fifth and sixth centuries, when Britain had ceased to be a part of the Roman Empire, is poorly understood. Roman-style administration seems to have continued for a time, but eventually new forms of governance and power emerged. One identifiable characteristic of this new political system was the reoccupation of some of the county's Iron Age hillforts and the refurbishment of their defences. Excavations at Cadbury Castle show that it was an important political centre at this time. Within the strengthened defences there was a large hall built in the sixth century. The works were probably carried out at the instigation of a local warlord or king. Whilst resorting to such places may in part have been a response to local tensions, it is thought that the primary reason was the threat from the expansion of the Anglo-Saxon kingdoms further east.

It is in this context that the legends of King Arthur emerged. Since at least the fifteenth century traditions have associated Cadbury Castle with Arthur's Camelot. Whether there is any truth in these stories or not, they do characterise a period when the South West was attempting to repulse Anglo-Saxon invaders.

An Anglo-Saxon hall at Shapwick

Evidence for buildings of Anglo-Saxon date in Somerset is rare. Most were of timber construction and have therefore not survived. Excavations at Shapwick did reveal postholes relating to a large timber building measuring some 16.5m long and 7m wide. The building probably had walls of wattle and daub in between the timber uprights.

The roof is presumed to have been thatched. Whilst no internal features, such as a hearth, had survived, this building is thought to have been a hall rather than a barn. The building probably dates from the seventh or eighth century and could have been used by a reeve or steward when visiting this part of the Glastonbury Abbey estate.

Workshops at Athelney

Alfred became King of the West Saxons in 871 when he was in his early twenties. From the beginning he faced Viking attempts to invade his kingdom. In January 878 one such invasion of Wessex took Alfred by surprise. The Vikings overran much of his kingdom and Alfred was driven into hiding at Athelney where he built a stronghold. Channel 4's *Time Team* focused on the 'island' of Athelney in 1993 and 2003. They demonstrated that pre-existing Iron Age defences were re-fortified in the later ninth century. Within the defences there was evidence for workshops where smithing and metalworking took place, almost certainly in preparation for Alfred's fight back against the Vikings.

Time Team filming on the site of Athelney Abbey in 2003. The camera is focused on the late Robin Bush, Victor Ambrus and Tony Robinson. (Photograph by Pauline Rook)

Guthrum surrenders to King Alfred

Early in May 878 Alfred mounted a counter-attack against the Vikings. He travelled from his stronghold at Athelney to 'Egbert's Stone', in east Somerset, where he was joined by the men of Somerset, Wiltshire and part of Hampshire. Alfred's army put the Vikings to flight in a battle at Edington in Wiltshire. The Vikings retreated to their stronghold at Chippenham where, after a siege lasting a fortnight, they surrendered. Peace was made and the invaders swore to leave Wessex. The agreement was sealed three weeks later when Guthrum, leader of the Vikings, joined Alfred at Aller, near Athelney, and was baptised. A few days later Alfred honoured Guthrum and his companions at Wedmore with the presentation of gifts. Alfred's successful defence of Wessex led in time to the formation of a unified kingdom of the English.

Alfred's time at Athelney generated three popular legends, all of which were established by the eleventh century. The best known is the story of Alfred and the cakes. According to this legend Alfred arrived at Athelney in disguise and took refuge in a swineherd's cottage. One day the swineherd's wife asked Alfred to watch over some cakes she was baking. He was distracted by the serious issues his kingdom was facing, allowed the cakes to burn and was duly scolded.

Alfred burning the cakes

Bishop Asser, Alfred's biographer

Asser was a monk of St David's in Wales, who entered King Alfred's service and eventually became bishop of Sherborne. His *Life of King Alfred*, reputedly written in 893, is an account of the king's activities in peace and war.

Alfred did not forget the refuge that Athelney had provided to him when his kingdom seemed lost. He founded a monastery of Benedictine monks there in gratitude to God for the Viking defeat. Asser provides a description of Athelney Abbey: surrounded by swampy, impassable and extensive marshland and groundwater on every side. It cannot be reached in any way except by punts or by a causeway which has been built by protracted labour between two fortresses [Athelney and Lyng]. In this monastery he gathered monks of various nationalities from every quarter, and assembled them there.'

Although it had an illustrious beginning, Athelney Abbey was always a small monastic house. It was overshadowed by the wealth and importance of Glastonbury Abbey which lay just 18km away. At the time of Domesday Book in 1086 Athelney had an annual value of just £20 compared with Glastonbury Abbey's £800. In its final years the abbey was burdened by debt, amounting in 1536 to £904. In 1534 there were twelve monks in addition to the abbot, a total that had been stable for some decades. But when Athelney Abbey was finally dissolved by Henry VIII in 1539, only six monks were left. Stone from the abbey buildings was removed for use elsewhere and nothing now remains above ground. In the foreground are excavations by Time Team in 2003 which revealed part of the monastic cemetery. The monument in the background was erected on the site of the abbey in 1801. (Photograph by Pauline Rook)

King Alfred has a special place in Somerset's history. He is commemorated in stained-glass windows in churches at Taunton, East Lyng, Aller and Wedmore. This stained-glass widow in St Bartholomew's church, East Lyng, was installed in about 1900. The Alfred Jewel is incorporated into the king's crown. During Queen Victoria's reign Alfred was venerated as the founder of the British Empire.

LYNG.
King Alfred's Millenary, 1901.
U. A. O. D.

The United Ancient Order of Druids Lodge 760 had their 'lodge room' at the Rose and Crown, East Lyng. The lodge was also known as the 'King Alfred the Great' lodge. They had a special gathering in August 1901 to mark the millenary of Alfred's death when members of the lodge wore druid-style clothing and false beards. They are easily recognisable amongst those present in this photograph of the event. The lodge put money raised at this event towards a new banner which featured a scene of Alfred burning the cakes.

CASTLES, ABBEYS, VILLAGES AND FIELDS

The Middle Ages saw the growth of towns and villages and of large baronial estates consisting of many manors. Great lords built not only castles but also churches and religious houses.

The Christian faith was a powerful force in medieval Somerset. Parish churches proliferated and were often buildings of great architectural quality. Many contained fine wall paintings, stained glass, furnishings and vestments. Most of this rich artistic legacy was destroyed during the Reformation in the 1540s and later.

Numerous religious houses were established in the county. Even the smallest monastic houses were important locally as centres of learning and charity. Some monasteries, such as Glastonbury Abbey, became rich landowners and had a powerful influence on the county's economy, landscape and settlement development.

Bridgwater Castle

The arrival of the Normans in Somerset was marked not least by the construction of castles. The earliest Norman castles were of 'motte and bailey' type. They consisted of a large earth mound (the motte) which had a timber tower on top and an area defended by banks and ditches (the bailey) which would have contained buildings. Later castles, such as Stogursey Castle and Taunton Castle, were stone built.

Bridgwater Castle was built in 1200 by William Brewer, an exceptionally wealthy man, after he was granted the lordship of the town by King John. The castle was rectangular in plan and lay on the west bank of the River Parrett. In about 1400 buildings within the inner bailey included chambers for estate officials, a kitchen, a cellar, a horse mill and a dungeon. Apart from a section of the water gate and a length of wall, nothing now survives of this substantial building above ground. Adjacent to the castle was the medieval bridge that gave the town its name.

Bridgwater grew to become an important port in the Middle Ages. Exports included woollen cloth, grain and hides. Substantial quantities of wine from France were imported.

Victor at Stogursey Castle with the archaeologist Bob Croft. A motte and bailey castle was built at Stogursey for the de Courcy family in the late eleventh or early twelfth century. The castle was given a stone curtain wall in about 1300. In 1459 the castle was burnt down by the Yorkists during the Wars of the Roses and it remained in a ruinous state until the Landmark Trust carried out restoration work in the 1980s. The building in the background dates from the seventeenth century and stands on the site of the castle's gatehouse. Today it serves as a holiday let. (Photograph by Justin Owen)

The Murder of Thomas Becket

Somerset people have on occasion played significant roles in major events. So it was on 29 December 1170 when Thomas Becket, Archbishop of Canterbury, was murdered in his cathedral. The event caused outrage across Europe. The relationship between Henry II and his archbishop had irretrievably broken down in 1164. Various attempts were made to reconcile the two men but to no avail. Tradition has it that Henry, whilst in a rage in Normandy in December 1170, uttered the words 'Will no one rid me of this turbulent priest?' Whatever the words may actually have been, they were taken as a royal command by four knights who set out to confront the archbishop at Canterbury. Their intention was almost certainly not to murder Becket but events very quickly got out of control. Three of the four knights actively involved in Becket's death came from Somerset and Devon. The first to strike with his sword was the ringleader Reginald Fitzurse of Williton in Somerset. Next was William de Tracy of Bradninch in Devon. The third and fatal blow was struck by Richard Brito of Sampford Brett in Somerset. The four knights were condemned to fourteen years' exile in the Holy Land but all were dead within five years.

Dismantling a farmstead at Shapwick

Prior to the tenth century, settlement in the parish of Shapwick, as elsewhere in Somerset, was dispersed so there was no village. Probably around the middle of the tenth century plots were laid out and a new village created. The dispersed farmsteads would have been dismantled and their components re-used wherever possible in the new buildings. Rather than locate the village close to the existing church, a site some distance to the west was chosen. We cannot be certain of the reasons, but it might have been due to there being a better supply of water.

Shapwick church and *curia* buildings

Shapwick's original church was located nearly 1km to the east of the subsequently established village and was dedicated to St Andrew. Geophysical survey and excavation have shown that it was of unusual design with a central tower. In order to manage its estates Glastonbury Abbey needed local bases to act as administrative centres. Their day-to-day running was the responsibility of local lay officials, the key ones being bailiff, reeve and steward. The responsibilities of these officials extended to the wider Glastonbury Abbey estates and as a consequence they were only at Shapwick periodically. Facilities were provided so that when at Shapwick they had somewhere to stay. The buildings were located within an enclosure adjacent to the church and included a hall, stables, detached kitchen and dovecote. As well as providing somewhere to stay, these premises would also have been used for official business such as the collection of dues and rents. This scene shows the old church and the abbey's administrative facilities, or *curia*, in about 1250.

The position of the early church well away from Shapwick village was clearly considered inconvenient because in the 1320s a petition was filed for a new church to be built within the village. Approval was given in January 1329 and the new church, dedicated to St Mary, was completed in about two and a half years.

The Knights Templar were a religious military order of knighthood established In the early eleventh century shortly after the First Crusade. They were religious men who carried swords. Originally founded to protect Christian pilgrims to the Holy Land, the order assumed greater military duties during the twelfth century. Its prominence and growing wealth provoked opposition from rival orders. Falsely accused of blasphemy and blamed for Crusader failures in the Holy Land, the order was ended by King Philip IV of France in the early fourteenth century.

Templecombe was the only preceptory of the Knights Templar in Somerset. The manor was given to the Order by Serlo Fitz Odo in 1185. The Templar Preceptor was responsible for managing the Order's estates in the West Country, admitting new members to the Order and training men and horses for service in the Crusades. Following the termination of the Order, William de Burton, the preceptor at Templecombe, and knights John de Aley and Walter de Rokele were committed to the Tower of London. Others were assigned to various monastic houses, including Glastonbury, Muchelney and Taunton, to spend the rest of their days in confinement.

Knights Templar at Templecombe

Bishop Ralph of Shrewsbury and the Black Death

Ralph of Shrewsbury, Bishop of Bath and Wells, has been regarded as an exemplary medieval bishop, and in his lifetime he gained a reputation for sanctity. He regularly travelled round his diocese and sought to improve the standards of the clergy. From the autumn of 1348 to the early summer of 1349 Bishop Ralph's diocese was devastated by the great plague, known as the Black Death. He retreated to his favourite residence at Wiveliscombe and directed the affairs of the diocese from there. In January 1349 he issued a mandate concerning confession for those who were sick. In the absence of a priest they might confess to a layman and, if necessary, to a woman.

There was considerable mortality amongst the clergy at the time of the Black Death. The abbeys of Athelney and Muchelney both lost their abbots. The number of monks at Glastonbury fell from eighty to forty. Half the population of Bridgwater succumbed. Overall the county may have lost one third of its inhabitants. There was no treatment for the plague and victims usually succumbed within 2–4 days of contracting the disease.

Nether Adber

The south-east of Somerset contains many deserted medieval villages. The reasons for the abandonment of these sites varied. Some were probably deserted as a consequence of the Black Death, but the desertion of others was almost certainly due to economic changes. The deserted settlement of Nether Adber survives as well-preserved earthworks. The house of the lord of the manor, fishponds, a chapel, the lines of village streets and rectangular buildings and perhaps a dovecote can be identified. Beyond the village earthworks there is some ridge-and-furrow, the remains of medieval strip fields. A survey dated 1562 lists only one person living in Nether Adber. Here, at least, desertion post-dated the Black Death.

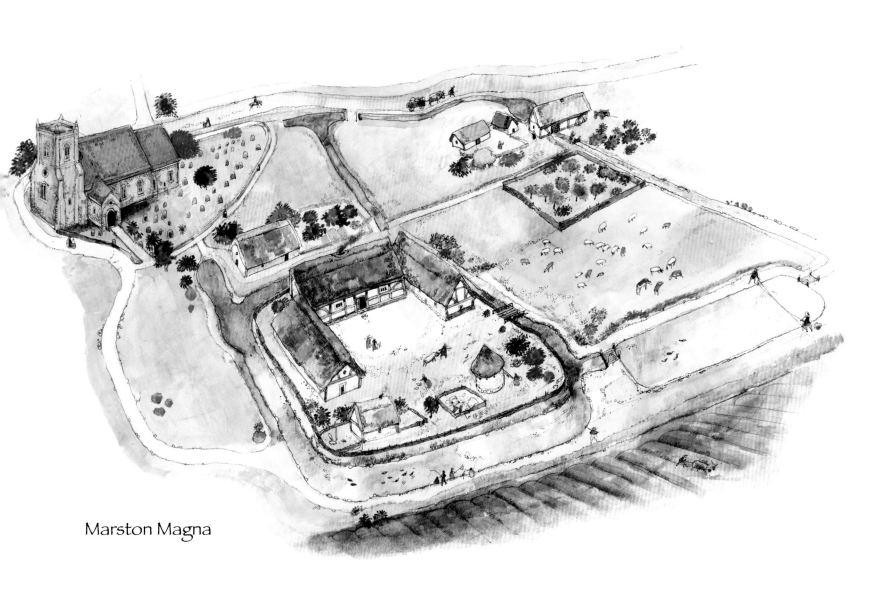

Marston Magna

At Marston Magna, just 1km from Nether Adber, are earthworks relating to a deserted moated site. The rectangular moat and two fishponds can be identified. The moat may have surrounded a grand house built of wood or cob belonging to the lord of the manor. Fishponds were both a status symbol and a source of fresh fish and waterfowl.

Ploughing the land at Stogursey in about 1450

The medieval landscape of Somerset is characterised by its pattern of small market towns, villages, hamlets and farmsteads with their associated field systems. Villages dominate the central and eastern part of the county, whereas hamlets and dispersed farms are more characteristic of west Somerset.

The Domesday Book of 1086 records that there were over forty households in Stogursey and amongst the population were seven slaves. There was land for 15 plough teams. There were also 150 acres of meadow, 19 acres of pasture, 100 acres of woodland, 29 cattle, 10 pigs, 250 sheep and a mill. By the middle of the fifteenth century Stogursey was a thriving small market town with a priory, a market place and a substantial parish church. Surrounding the village were strip fields which would have been farmed in common. The products of each season were carefully looked after to ensure that the community could survive the winter. This scene depicts a plough team of oxen working together to get the ploughing completed in time. Horses were not widely used for ploughing until post-medieval times.

The execution of Abbot Richard Whiting

Glastonbury Abbey was once the wealthiest monastic house in England. The Abbot of Glastonbury lived in considerable splendour and wielded tremendous power. Richard Whiting became Abbot in 1525. The first ten years of Whiting's rule were prosperous and peaceful. He was a sober and caring spiritual leader and a good manager of the abbey's day-to-day life. Contemporary accounts show that Whiting was held in very high esteem. About 100 monks lived in the enclosed monastery, where the sons of the nobility and gentry were educated before going on to university.

As a consequence of Henry VIII's dissolution of the monasteries Glastonbury was the only monastery left in Somerset by the autumn of 1539. Abbot Whiting refused to surrender the abbey. On 19 September of that year the royal commissioners arrived there without warning on the orders of Thomas Cromwell, presumably to find faults and thus facilitate the abbey's closure. Whiting, by then about 78 years old, was sent to the Tower of London so that Cromwell might examine him himself. Some sort of trial apparently took place at Wells on Friday 14 November and he was convicted of 'robbing Glastonbury church'. The next day he was taken to Glastonbury with two of his monks, John Thorne and Roger James, where all three were fastened upon hurdles and dragged by horses to the top of Glastonbury Tor. There they were hanged, drawn and quartered. Whiting's head was fastened over the west gate of the now deserted abbey and his limbs were exposed at Wells, Bath, Ilchester and Bridgwater.

When it was dissolved in 1539 Glastonbury Abbey's buildings were plundered and this once magnificent complex of buildings quickly became ruinous. George Arnald's painting of circa 1810 presents the abbey as a romanticised symbol of the past.

A Rebellious County

Somerset has been drawn into several rebellions of national significance, notably those of Perkin Warbeck in 1497 and the Duke of Monmouth in 1685. It also had an important part in the English Civil War which began in 1642

The rebellious Perkin Warbeck

The fifteenth century was marked by the dynastic struggles between the houses of York and Lancaster. Perkin Warbeck was probably born in Tournai in France. Whilst in Cork in 1491 Warbeck began to impersonate Richard, Duke of York, second son of Edward IV, who had disappeared in 1483 together with his elder brother, Edward V – the two 'Princes in the Tower'. Warbeck's aim was to take the throne from Henry VII. With the support of a variety of patrons, including Maximilian, king of the Romans, and James IV of Scotland, Warbeck continued the impersonation until his downfall.

Warbeck's final attempt on the throne of Henry VII took place in 1497. In May of that year heavy taxation sparked rebellion in Cornwall which soon spread to Somerset and beyond. Warbeck saw this as an opportunity and landed in Cornwall on 7 September. His force of about 300 rapidly grew and they advanced eastwards. By the time they laid siege to Exeter his followers were perhaps 8,000 strong, though most were peasants 'never exercised in war nor marciall feates, but only with the spade and shovell'. Rebuffed at Exeter by the Earl of Devon, they continued to Taunton, arriving on 19 September. The approach of Henry's army threw Warbeck and his army into confusion. In the early hours of 21 September Warbeck and his closest followers made their escape, only to be recognised and captured at Beaulieu Abbey.

Henry VII came to Taunton Castle to question Warbeck in person on 5 October. Warbeck admitted that he was a pretender when asked whether he recognised any of the court members present. Had he been Duke Richard he would have known some of them; as an imposter he did not. He was sentenced to the Tower of London for life. In the event he became involved in a plot to free his fellow prisoner, the Earl of Warwick, and to escape himself. The plot was discovered and Warbeck was hanged at Tyburn. The failure of Warbeck's campaign marked the real end of the Wars of the Roses.

Civil War

Somerset gained a reputation as a rebellious county during the seventeenth century and endured great suffering in the Civil War and Monmouth Rebellion.

In 1642 Civil War broke out between the forces of Charles I and his Parliament. In Somerset loyalties were divided. Lord Poulett, Sir John Stawell, Sir William Portman and Sir Ralph Hopton were for the king and Sir John Horner, Alexander Popham and William Strode for Parliament. These divisions extended to families. Everyone was affected by the war. Crops were destroyed, cattle stolen and houses burned. It was one of the greatest disasters Somerset ever experienced.

During the Civil War many people hid their valuable possessions to protect them. Occasionally they were not recovered. This hoard of four silver spoons, a goblet and bell salt was buried for safety at Nether Stowey in the 1640s. Each piece carries the letters GAC, the initials of the unidentified married couple who owned them. For reasons unknown these valuable objects were not recovered from their place of concealment.

Taunton besieged

Most people living in Taunton were supporters of the Parliamentarian cause. However, in May 1643 the town fell into the hands of the Royalists. They remained in control for a year, by which time they had reduced the garrison to just eighty soldiers. They were no match for the Parliamentarian force sent to take Taunton under the command of Robert Blake. The Cavaliers surrendered on 5 June 1644 after a siege lasting just one week. In October 1644 a Royalist force of 3,000 men was sent to besiege and re-take the town. They bombarded the castle from the west and the town from the east. Blake and his soldiers held out and the day was saved by the arrival of a relief force which prompted the Royalist soldiers to withdraw.

Blake repaired and improved Taunton's defences. By 10 April 1645 the town was once again besieged. The Royalists were aware that their time was limited as a relief force would inevitably be sent. On 6 and 7 May an attack on the East Gate was fought off by the use of stones and boiling water. On 8 May the Royalists launched a violent onslaught on all fronts. Blake and his soldiers were forced back into the castle, the area of St Mary's and the market place. On 9 May, Blake received a demand that he surrender. His well-known response was that he had four pairs of boots and would eat three of them before giving in. On 11 May the relieving force arrived and once again the Royalists withdrew.

Fire starters

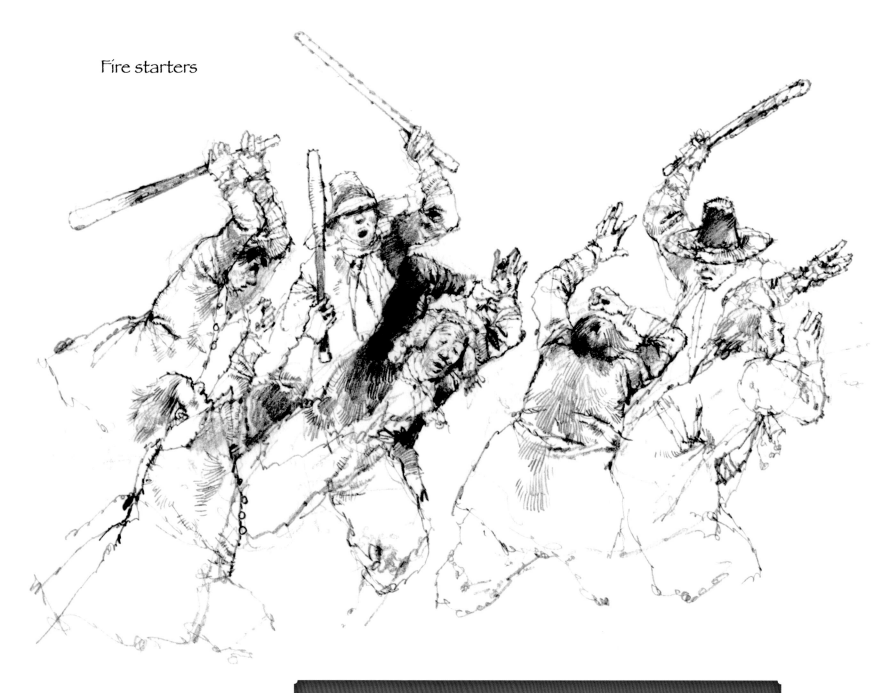

There were some Royalist supporters amongst the people of Taunton. Two men and a woman were caught trying to start fires in the town in order to assist the besiegers. They were killed by an angry mob and some of their accomplices were hanged.

Taunton paid a terrible price in May 1645 with at least 100 people killed, 200 wounded and two thirds of the town burnt down. A contemporary account described the scene: 'heaps of rubbish ... consumed houses ... Here a poor forsaken chimney, and there a little fragment of a wall.'

The events at Taunton were of more than local significance. They involved a considerable number of Royalist troops who would otherwise have been fighting for the king's cause at the Battle of Naseby on 14 June, the decisive battle in the defeat of Charles I.

Devastation in Taunton

The Battle of Langport

Following their victory at Naseby, the Parliamentarian New Model Army moved to the West Country in order to relieve Taunton which was once again besieged, this time by Lord Goring. Goring attempted a tactical withdrawal to the safety of Bridgwater and in the process he took up a position on high ground just outside Langport. Goring had split his forces, sending most of his artillery ahead towards Bridgwater. Although he held a strong position, Goring's forces were both outnumbered and outgunned, and any resistance soon crumbled during this battle on 10 July 1645. Defeat at Langport all but destroyed Royalist ambitions in the West Country. Two days later the Parliamentarian army, under the command of Sir Thomas Fairfax, laid siege to Bridgwater.

Christabella Wyndham was a particularly strong personality and she and her husband Edmund made the best use of opportunities at Court. They had ten children, six sons and four daughters, of whom all but one reached maturity. Christabella was chosen by Queen Henrietta Maria to be Lady Nurse to her son, the future King Charles II, and at a later date was reputedly his mistress.

Edmund Wyndham was in Bridgwater as governor when the Parliamentarian Sir Thomas Fairfax besieged the town in 1645. On 12 July Fairfax went to view the town's defences. He was seen from the walls and a gun was fired at him (legend says by Christabella Wyndham). Nobody was hit although the bullet was said to have passed close to Fairfax. Two attempts by Fairfax to negotiate an end to the conflict failed after Lady Wyndham, bearing her breasts, told his messenger: 'Tell your masters that the breast which gave suck to Prince Charles shall never be at their mercy; we will hold the town to the last.' Shortly before the final bombardment and fall of the town to the Parliamentarians, Fairfax gave the women and children two hours to leave. 'A whole regiment' of them came streaming out, including the stout-hearted Christabella. Shortly afterwards the garrison surrendered and Edmund was taken prisoner.

A defiant Christabella Wyndham

Edmund Wyndham was a leading figure in some of the key events in Somerset during the Civil War. In August 1644 he besieged Taunton, then held by Robert Blake. Wyndham was Governor of Bridgwater when the town fell to the Parliamentarians on 12 July 1645. Prior to the Civil War he had been MP for Bridgwater, a position to which he was once again elected in 1661 following the Restoration. He died in 1681 aged 80 years.

The Monmouth Rebellion

When Charles II returned in May 1660 to reclaim his throne there was widespread rejoicing. A member of the Poulett family of Hinton St George counted 142 celebratory bonfires within sight of Hinton House. The gentry, both Parliamentarian and Royalist, welcomed the Restoration. But early harmony was short-lived, especially as it became clear that Royalists wanted revenge, not reconciliation.

In Somerset towns and villages hundreds of people refused to accept the doctrines of the re-established Anglican Church and flocked instead to nonconformist conventicles. Nowhere was nonconformist support stronger than in Taunton. In the early 1680s government-approved persecution of dissenters increased. Disaffection grew rapidly. It was exacerbated as they contemplated the likely succession to the throne of Charles II's Catholic brother, James, Duke of York. Hopes and desires for a Protestant king lay with James, Duke of Monmouth, the king's favourite but illegitimate son.

When the Catholic James II succeeded to the throne in February 1685, Monmouth became the focus for Protestant opposition. He was in exile in Amsterdam at the time. Plans for a rebellion were quickly made, and on 11 June 1685 Monmouth landed at Lyme Regis with three ships and eighty followers. He hoped that the Protestant West Country would flock to join him in his attempt to take the throne. One of the most remarkable things about the Monmouth Rebellion is the amount known about many of the ordinary people who were involved.

James, Duke of Monmouth.

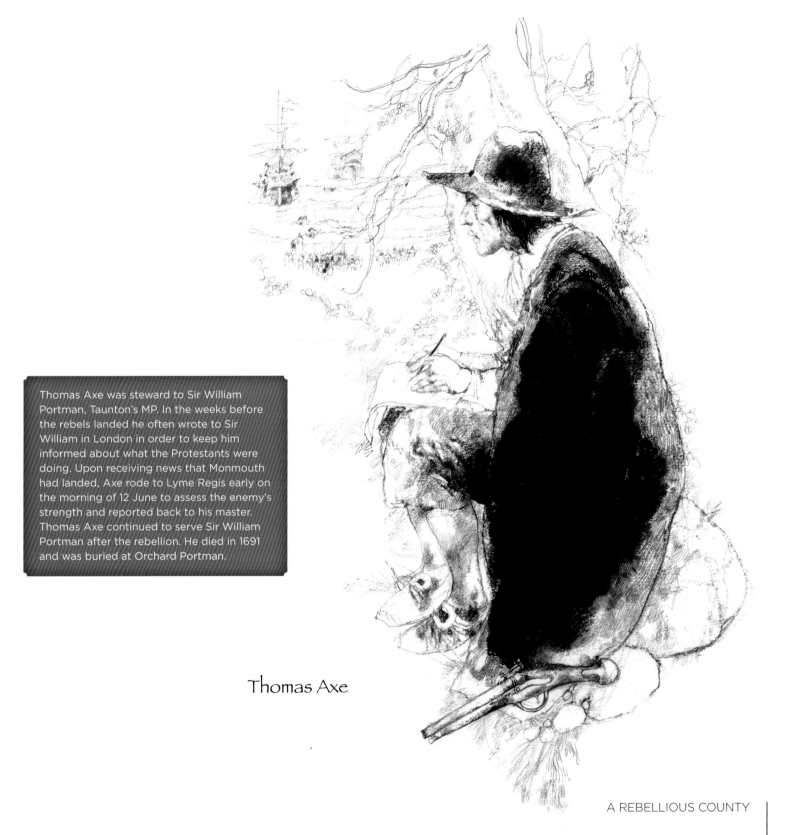

Thomas Axe was steward to Sir William Portman, Taunton's MP. In the weeks before the rebels landed he often wrote to Sir William in London in order to keep him informed about what the Protestants were doing. Upon receiving news that Monmouth had landed, Axe rode to Lyme Regis early on the morning of 12 June to assess the enemy's strength and reported back to his master. Thomas Axe continued to serve Sir William Portman after the rebellion. He died in 1691 and was buried at Orchard Portman.

Thomas Axe

After landing at Lyme Regis, Monmouth, marching under a banner bearing the words 'Fear Nothing But God', led his growing army through Axminster, Chard and Ilminster. Daniel Manning was a blacksmith's apprentice at a forge at Shoreditch, near Taunton, when the Duke of Monmouth's army rode past. He joined the rebels on their march in order to shoe their 'cattle and horses'. Manning later deserted Monmouth and joined the king's forces. He marched with them to Westonzoyland but because he had no weapons he did not fight in the Battle of Sedgemoor.

Daniel Manning

Mary Blake

Monmouth reached Taunton on 18 June and was greeted with wild enthusiasm in the flower-strewn streets. Two days later at Taunton Market Cross he was proclaimed king. The twenty-seven 'maids of Taunton' presented him with flags for his troops and Mary Blake, a schoolmistress, gave him a Bible and sword. After the Battle of Sedgemoor, Mary Blake and twelve of her pupils were arrested. Mary was imprisoned in Dorchester Gaol, where she died of smallpox.

The Battle of Sedgemoor

Monmouth's army left Taunton on 21 June and spent an exhausting week marching across the Mendip Hills towards Bristol. At first it seemed as if the rebellion might succeed, but when the Royal army approached the West Country, Monmouth retreated to Bridgwater. He decided on a surprise night attack after receiving news that the king's forces, camped near Westonzoyland, were poorly defended. However, after a series of mishaps the alarm was raised amongst the Royal army.

Monmouth's rebellion against King James ended in crushing defeat at the Battle of Sedgemoor on 6 July 1685. Contemporary figures for the numbers killed during the battle were twenty-seven royal soldiers and around 700 rebels. A thousand more rebels were killed as they fled.

Hundreds of rebels were captured and put on trial. The Bloody Assizes began at Winchester on 25 August 1685 and continued at Dorchester, Exeter, Taunton and Wells. Over 1,400 prisoners were tried and at least 300 rebels were sentenced to be hanged, drawn and quartered. Nearly 750 were transported to the West Indies.

The last of the battle was still being fought as the Duke of Monmouth made his escape from Sedgemoor. He was hoping to escape to France. Though disguised in country clothes, he was soon captured near Ringwood in Dorset. His fate was inevitable, and on 15 July 1685 he was beheaded on Tower Hill, London.

This spy-glass belonged to William Sparke of Chedzoy, near Bridgwater. From the top of Chedzoy church tower he used it to watch the king's army gathering at Westonzoyland. Sparke sent a farm worker to tell the Duke of Monmouth that the Royalist camp was poorly defended. As a result, Monmouth decided that a surprise night attack could succeed. The disastrous Battle of Sedgemoor followed.

Lord Chief Justice Judge Jeffreys presided at the Bloody Assizes. The assizes held at Taunton Castle took place on 18 and 19 September 1685 when 514 prisoners were tried. Of these 146 were sentenced to be hanged, drawn and quartered. Following the overthrow of James II in 1688 Jeffreys was imprisoned in the Tower of London, where he died on 18 April 1689 from kidney disease.

Charles Speke first met the Duke of Monmouth when he visited Somerset in 1680. He stayed in Speke's father's house at Whitelackington for a short time whilst on a tour through the West Country. Monmouth was a charming man and large crowds welcomed him wherever he went. Charles Speke didn't see him again until Monmouth arrived in Ilminster market place with his army in June 1685. Having met previously the two men shook hands. Speke did not join the rebellion, but his handshake was later enough to have him condemned. Judge Jeffreys sentenced him to death for treason at the Wells Assizes in September 1685. Speke was hanged in Ilminster market place before a great and silent crowd.

Charles Speke

John Hucker

When Monmouth reached Taunton with his army on 18 June 1685 he stayed at John Hucker's house in East Street in the town centre. Hucker, a sergemaker, joined his army as an officer and led a troop of horse at the Battle of Sedgemoor. He was accused by some of having fired the pistol that warned the king's army of the night-time attack at Sedgemoor, something that was almost certainly not true. John Hucker was tried at the Taunton assizes and on 30 September was hanged from a gallows on Taunton's Cornhill.

Henry Pitman only came to Taunton out of curiosity to see Monmouth, but in the excitement he was persuaded to join his army. He was a medical man and treated wounded soldiers from both sides. When the battle was over he was arrested and imprisoned in Ilchester gaol.

Pitman was sentenced to transportation and sailed for Barbados from Weymouth, where he was destined to work for a plantation owner. All turned out well for Henry Pitman. After many adventures he eventually returned to England and was pardoned in 1687.

Henry Pitman

Benjamin Hewling

Benjamin Hewling was from London and served as a cavalry officer in Monmouth's army. He didn't fight at Sedgemoor, having been sent to Minehead to collect some cannon. Nevertheless, he was still arrested and tried before Judge Jeffreys at Taunton Castle. Hewling's family did all that they could to save him from the gallows. His sister even pleaded with the king to spare his life but to no avail. Benjamin Hewling, aged 22 years, was hanged at Taunton and buried in St Mary's churchyard. His brother William was hanged at Lyme Regis.

Edward Hobbes

Edward Hobbes was Somerset's High Sheriff in 1685. His responsibilities included making sure that the execution of the prisoners was properly carried out. When the rebels were executed in Bath he ordered that a cauldron be provided for boiling their heads and quarters. Hobbes served for a year as Somerset's High Sheriff until December 1685. He came from Stogursey and died in 1693. We cannot know what memories he carried to the grave.

Mary Bridge

Colonel Kirke presented Mary Bridge with the sword she used to kill the Royalist officer while protecting her mother. The sword passed down through the generations until being given to the Somerset Archaeological and Natural History Society in 1932.

After terrible suffering in the Civil War and the Monmouth Rebellion, Somerset wanted peace, stability and a Protestant king. In 1688 Somerset gentry supported William of Orange when he claimed the throne from his Catholic uncle, James II. The 'Glorious Revolution' succeeded almost without bloodshed and religion never again so divided the people of England.

The Modern Era

Between 1550 and 1850 the rural landscape of Somerset began to take on its modern form as the remnants of the medieval field systems were enclosed to form paddocks, orchards, closes and meadows. The Somerset Levels and Moors were largely enclosed with ditches or rhynes between about 1770 and 1840 to form the rectangular pattern of fields still visible today. The population of the county increased and small market towns developed and flourished. This period also saw the development of large country estates and the creation of extensive parks and gardens such as Burton Pynsent and Ston Easton Park.

During the late eighteenth and early nineteenth century canals such as the Bridgwater and Taunton Canal gave interior parts of the county access to the sea for the transport of goods. Money from tolls enabled major road improvements. By 1840 railways were developing across the county. Over the next fifty years these transport improvements unlocked rural Somerset. Among the many impacts of these developments was the growth of tourism which is so important to the county today.

Although not generally regarded as an industrial county, Somerset has a remarkably varied industrial past with brick and tile making in Bridgwater and Wellington, an art bronze foundry at Frome, the British Cellophane factory at Bridgwater and Westland Helicopters in Yeovil. Most visible today are the nuclear power stations at Hinkley Point.

Shapwick, a large parish in central Somerset, has been subject to an exceptional programme of archaeological and historical research. In the 1970s and '80s the Somerset Levels Project focused on the wetland area of Shapwick where remarkable discoveries, including the Sweet Track, were made. Between 1989 and 1999 the Shapwick Project carried out an intensive programme of archaeological and historical research on the Shapwick dryland. Together, these two projects make Shapwick the most thoroughly studied parish in Somerset.

The late Mick Aston was one of the directors of the Shapwick Project. In this and many other ways Mick contributed enormously to our understanding of Somerset's archaeology and history. (Photograph by Pauline Rook)

Shapwick House and formal gardens in the seventeenth century

In the mid-1600s Shapwick House passed into the possession of the Rolle family. They had a special interest in horticulture and re-modelled the gardens to the north of their house to include a walled lawn, raised gravel paths, two ornamental ponds and a banqueting house. The latter served as a stopping-off point for refreshments and rest during a walk or carriage ride around the estate. Formality and symmetry were the fashion of the time. The Rolle family carried out further landscaping work close to Shapwick House in the 1700s, notably the creation of Shapwick Park to the south of the house.

By the end of the eighteenth century much of the medieval open field system had been enclosed. The new hedge-surrounded fields would have created a very different landscape from that of previous centuries. The process was not without its problems. In May 1749 John Walter of Shapwick was presented before a court for illegally fencing a piece of land. He had presumably taken land that was not his. Walter returned to face the court in May 1752, this time for planting trees on the same piece of land. He seems to have been trying to establish a permanent hedge line and a stock-proof barrier.

Planting a hedgerow at Shapwick

Shapwick Old Bakery

In the nineteenth century farming and agricultural work were the predominant occupations amongst the inhabitants of Shapwick but other people had occupations that are no longer pursued there today. For men these included footman, shoemaker, stonemason, blacksmith, tailor and sawyer and for women they included dairywoman, house servant, kitchen maid and needlewoman.

There was also a baker. This drawing shows the Old Bakery in the later nineteenth century. William Thier Pitcher was the baker throughout most of the second half of the nineteenth century. Excavations in the garden of the Old Bakery revealed the graves of several dogs. Marks on the leg bones of one of the dogs suggested that it had spent much of its life chained up.

Friendly Societies were of enormous importance in nineteenth-century Somerset. They were local self-help organisations that did much to mitigate the worst effects of economic problems faced by their members at a time when there were few other welfare benefits. Those joining paid a weekly subscription and in return received financial support at times of illness or unemployment.

Even the cost of funerals could be covered. Friendly Societies had an annual celebration or 'Club Walk' around the village or parish that included a service in the church or chapel followed by a meal. The club's banner was carried high and members held staffs at the top of which were the society's distinctive brasses. The walks, often accompanied by the village band, were important social occasions.

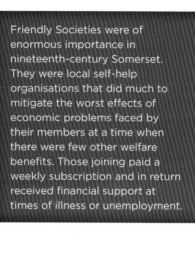

A Friendly Society walk

In the eighteenth century, England's road system was transformed by the formation of turnpike trusts. These organisations financed road improvements by levying tolls. In the early nineteenth century a turnpike trust created a new road through Shapwick. There, as elsewhere, accommodation in the form of a toll house was built for the collector of the tolls. The census shows that the toll keeper at Shapwick was more often than not a woman.

Shapwick toll house

Benhole Farm

At the beginning of the twentieth century farming in Somerset was dominated by dairying and stock rearing. As a consequence, some 77 per cent of farmland was permanent grass. There were a quarter of a million cattle and half a million sheep. The size of the average farm was just 60 acres and very few exceeded 300 acres. The situation changed with the First World War and the need for wheat. Some 34,000 acres were ploughed up to grow cereals for food.

Benhole Farm, Stogursey, was the home of the Wills family from 1912 to 1928. They kept cattle, sheep, chickens, geese and turkeys on their 200-acre farm. The land extended to the coast. Sometimes cattle and sheep wandered too close to the cliffs and fell to their deaths. Benhole Farm was occasionally in the news. In 1937 a man set off to travel by boat from Weston-super-Mare to Clevedon. A gale sprang up and he drifted all night. He was driven ashore at 5 o'clock the next morning convinced that he had landed on the Welsh coast. The man made his way to the nearest house and was most surprised to discover that it was Benhole Farm in Somerset. The farm no longer exists, having burnt down. The site now lies within the area of Hinkley Point C power station.

Peat digging

Peat has been cut for fuel in Somerset since Roman times. Until the second half of the twentieth century the work was all done by hand. By the end of the nineteenth century the usual method was to dig the peat in long lines. The peat was cut as blocks (known as 'mumps') using long-handled spades. 'Mumps' were cut into three smaller 'turves' which then had to be dried. First, they were put into small stacks called 'hyles' and a little later into large, round-topped piles of around 1,000 'turves' called 'ruckles'. The work of digging peat was carried out by men but the building of 'hyles' and 'ruckles' was frequently done by women and children. The work was extremely hard. Cider was an essential part of the working day.

Once dried, the peat blocks were used as domestic fuel. Locally they were delivered by horse and cart or by water in flat-bottomed peat boats. Some peat was taken further afield by train.

Roger Rogers recalled his parents digging peat in the early 1960s in an oral history recording made by the late Ann Heeley:

... two men could dig about five thousand blocks a day, that was the average that they would have to dig to actually earn their money. You could earn £2 a week. It was a good wage compared with farm labourers. It was long hours and long days. Father used to start anything from five and six in the morning ... [Mother] would put the peat into rows.

Fishing has long been important on the Somerset coast. As well as the traditional forms of fishing the county has seen some more unusual activity. Oysters were important at Porlock Weir as early as the beginning of the eighteenth century. The beds were at their most prolific in the later nineteenth century. The oysters were gathered by trailing drag nets from sloops. Once collected they were kept in a walled-in area on the beach, known as a perch, near the point of low tide. Remains of the perches still survive at Porlock Weir. As oysters were only gathered between the months of September to April the boats would presumably have been used for general fishing at other times. Oyster dredging seems to have ended in the early decades of the twentieth century when the beds were no longer productive, reputedly as the result of fishermen coming down from Colchester and Whitstable and decimating the beds.

Oyster dredging at Porlock Weir

In April 2014 a local community pilot scheme began at Porlock Weir to test the viability of oyster farming. Ten thousand seed oysters were placed at the low watermark. Conditions were ideal for the Pacific oyster and the business, Porlock Bay Oysters, is proving to be a great success. The oysters are reared on iron trestles which are exposed when the tide goes out. Boats are therefore no longer part of the process. Here oysters are being gathered in 2016. (Photograph by Pauline Rook)

Mud-horse fishing

When the tide goes out on the Somerset coast, it leaves long flat beaches of fine sand and mud, which can be treacherous, and here a distinctive method of fishing evolved. The fishermen used 'mud-horses' to cross the difficult landscape when the tide went out. They worked rather like sledges. The fisherman lies across the upper frame of the mud-horse, so that his weight is spread much more evenly over the surface of the mud, preventing him from sinking. He propels himself by a kicking-out action, rather than an upright walking motion. His fishing gear is hooked to the frame of the mud-horse or is carried in baskets fitted to the frame. In this way, a man on a mud-horse can skim across the mudflats much faster and more safely than someone on foot.

Mud-horses were used at low tide to gather and transport fish caught in nets held up by stakes driven into the mud. The main catch was shrimps, but fish such as cod and whiting could be caught in winter, and skate and sea bass in summer. As recently as fifty years ago, this way of life was carried on by a number of families along the Somerset coast, but now there is only one mud-horse fisherman left – Adrian Sellick of Stolford. It is likely that his will be the last generation of Somerset mud-horse fishermen. This drawing shows mud-horse fishing in about 1970, with construction work on Hinkley Point B underway in the background.

The Sellick family fish shop at Stolford in 2009.

West Somerset Mineral Railway

Iron ore has been periodically mined on the Brendon Hills for the past 2,000 years. Mining on an industrial scale occurred from the 1850s to early 1880s, inspired by a high demand for wrought iron with correspondingly high prices. The iron ore was taken to the harbour at Watchet and shipped to Newport in South Wales, from where it was taken to one of the Ebbw Vale Company's smelting works. The West Somerset Mineral Railway was built between 1857 and 1864. Although the railway carried passengers, its primary purpose was to carry the ore from the mines to Watchet, a journey of 11 miles. By the late 1860s over 200 men from Somerset and Cornwall were working in the mines and on the railway. Activity at this level was short-lived. Cheap imports of iron from Spain made mining on the Brendon Hills uneconomic. Work ceased in 1883, although the railway continued to operate for passenger traffic until 1898.

Figure of Justice on the Old Bailey

John Webb Singer established the Frome Art Metal Works in 1848 in response to the demand for brasswork in churches. The company was to go by various names and is perhaps best known as J.W. Singer & Sons Ltd. In 1888 an art bronze foundry was added to the business. It proved to be highly successful. They were responsible for some of the country's best-known bronze castings including Boudica and her daughters in a war chariot near Westminster Bridge, London, the figure of Justice above the Old Bailey and the statue of Alfred the Great in Winchester. They also produced many art bronze castings on a smaller scale, including war memorials following the end of the First World War.

View of the interior of Singers' foundry shortly after the end of the First World War.

Autumn is carnival season in Somerset. The tradition is said to go back 400 years. There are some twenty-two carnivals held across the county. They involve months of planning and preparation. Hundreds of people take part in the creation of floats and costumes and as performers. Tens of thousands of people turn out to watch and enjoy them. Bridgwater Carnival is the highlight. It is said to attract 150,000 people and to be the largest illuminated carnival in the world.

Today's carnivals are mainly held in Somerset's towns, but in the past villages often also put on carnivals. Modern floats are notable for their lights and sounds; in the past they were much simpler and often involved people walking dressed in costume or travelling aboard waggons.

In 1890, excursion trains brought people from Bristol, Bath, Taunton, Evercreech, Glastonbury, Burnham on Sea and elsewhere to the Bridgwater Guy Fawkes Carnival. The parade included 'a gang of Bulgarians', 'an Oriental lady, costly attired, accompanied in a carriage by a Hermit', 'Prince Kantakehispantsoff' and 'King Charles I' who were followed by clowns in carts, Mexican Brigands, African chiefs and the warship *Victory* with Admiral Nelson. Preparations were needed before the start of the Bridgwater Carnival in 1921 and included erecting wooden barricades in front of shop windows and enclosing the statue of Admiral Blake in his 'little wooden hut' owing to the close proximity of the bonfire.

In November 1929 a special excursion train ran from London to take people to the Bridgwater Carnival. The fare was 8 shillings.

A Bridgwater carnival float in the early 1900s

Tourism is one of Somerset's most important industries. It began with the coming of the railways which gave people easy access to the coast. Towns such as Burnham on Sea, Highbridge and Minehead became favourite tourist destinations and underwent great changes as a consequence. The railway reached Minehead in 1874, which was relatively late, but the town became one of Somerset's most popular resorts.

Sea bathing became established in the nineteenth century. Bathing machines were commonly used to enable people to change into their swimwear and then enter the sea without being seen by others. Wheels enabled the bathing machines to be moved up and down the beach according to the state of the tide. They were often positioned in the sea so that the occupants could walk down the steps straight into the water. For much of the nineteenth century men and women were obliged to bathe separately on different parts of the beach.

Bathing machines were a common sight at Somerset's seaside resorts including Weston-super-Mare, Clevedon, Burnham on Sea and Minehead. At Weston-super-Mare they began to go out of use after a severe storm in 1903 when over 100 bathing machines were destroyed and not replaced. At Minehead, however, there was an insistence on their continued use until the mid-1930s.

Bathing machine at Minehead

Butlin's at Minehead

Billy Butlin opened his first holiday camp at Skegness in 1936. The promise was 'A week's holiday for a week's wages.' Holiday camps proved popular with families and more were opened. Butlin's, Minehead, was officially opened on 26 May 1962.

Entertainment was at the heart of the Butlin's offer and was led by the famous Redcoats. Butlin's was at the height of popularity in the 1970s. There was very significant investment in the Minehead site in the 1980s and '90s, including

the Skyline Pavilion which is the distinctive feature of Butlin's in the landscape. Butlin's, Minehead, continues to be a popular family holiday destination.

Until 1967 guests wore camp pin badges to show that they were part of the Butlin's 'club'. The badges demonstrated that the wearer was entitled to be on site and eligible to use facilities such as the camp bars. This badge was worn at Minehead in 1964.

The First World War profoundly affected Somerset. About one in ten of Somerset's male population of service age died in the war. Thousands of other people, in towns and villages, coped with refugees, wounded soldiers and food shortages and worked in support of the war effort.

Britain went to war on 4 August 1914 in response to Germany's invasion of Belgium. Within days recruiting meetings were taking place across Somerset and thousands of men volunteered. They often enlisted with friends or relatives so they could serve together. Soon the railway platforms of Somerset were crowded with soldiers leaving for war. Amongst them was 'C' Squadron of the West Somerset Yeomanry, seen here on their horses preparing to leave for Essex from Bridgwater on 12 August 1914. The West Somerset Yeomanry were dismounted in 1915. In September of that year they sailed from Liverpool to the Mediterranean, where they were to take part in the Gallipoli campaign.

The war devastated a generation. Many people, both soldiers and civilians, carried the burden of four destructive years until the end of their lives.

First World War: departing for France

Heinkel shot down at Charterhouse on Mendip

Following the outbreak of the Second World War on 3 September 1939 the lives of people across the county were to be dramatically affected once again. While thousands departed for distant battlefields, over the next six years those at home experienced food rationing and the blackout, evacuees and the Land Army girls, American soldiers and Home Guard patrols. The Somerset landscape also changed: 48,000 acres of grassland were ploughed up in order to grow more crops, concrete pillboxes were constructed, barricades were built at the entrances to towns and villages, obstacles such as iron stakes and piles of stones were placed on beaches, new airfields appeared and signposts were removed from the roads.

Somerset was not immune from the German air force. Over 60,000 bombs were dropped on the county. Most fell in open countryside but some were deadly. Thirty-five people died in Yeovil in October 1940 as the result of direct hits on two air-raid shelters.

Not all German planes returned home safely. The RAF was ready to intercept bombing raids and a number of German bombers were shot down over Somerset. They included three Heinkels on their way to bomb Cardiff Docks on 14 August 1940. The planes were brought down by Spitfires. One made a forced landing at Charterhouse on Mendip. The crew of five were taken prisoner, having first tried to set fire to the plane. A second Heinkel came down at Puriton, having jettisoned its bombs over the Somerset Levels. The third Heinkel came down in Bridgwater Bay with the loss of all five members of the crew.

For almost 2,000 years work has been undertaken to reclaim the wetlands of the Somerset Levels and Moors and prevent flooding by the sea and inland water. In spite of this enormous human endeavour the area has periodically been overwhelmed by water, most recently during the winter of 2013/14.

In the winter of 1929/30 537mm of rain fell, causing floods which lasted from December to February. Athelney and the surrounding area was very badly affected when the River Tone burst its banks. Nearly 200 families were made homeless and a number of houses collapsed. People were rescued from their homes by boat. Boats were also used to deliver food to those who refused to leave their houses. A Flood Relief Fund raised over £22,000 towards helping those affected.

Ruby Palmer was 9 years old at the time of the 1929 flood. Her memories are from an oral history recording made by the late Ann Heeley:

Oh dear, it was Sunday December 9th, we'd had a lot of rain and this particular Sunday the river was very high, very high … The river burst its banks … we stayed upstairs, we were up there for Christmas. The water [in the house] was up to two or three feet or more. [Press photographers] came out in a boat up the road and took our photograph hanging out the window.

Athelney floods in 1929/30

Somerset is still not immune from flooding, as was shown in the winter of 2013/14. Over 600 houses and 6,900 hectares of agricultural land were affected. As in 1929 rescue boats were used. This view looking towards the village of East Lyng shows the Isle of Athelney in the foreground. The nearest 'island' was the location of the fort built by King Alfred in 878 and of the abbey that he built following his defeat of the Danes. The photograph clearly demonstrates the strategic nature of the site in an era before the drainage of the Somerset Levels and Moors and resonates with Asser's description of Athelney Abbey in the late ninth century as 'surrounded by swampy, impassable and extensive marshland and groundwater on every side'. (Photograph by Historic England)

The twentieth century saw some remarkable archaeological discoveries in Somerset. None was more important than the Low Ham Roman mosaic. In 1937 farmer Herbert Cook went into one of his fields at Low Ham and discovered that a sheep had died. Rather than move the body he decided to bury it where it lay. In digging the grave Herbert discovered a fragment of earthenware tile that intrigued him. It was flat with combed decoration on one surface. On his next visit to the Somerset County Museum in Taunton he showed it to the curator, who identified it as part of a box-flue tile from a Roman central heating system. Herbert donated the tile to the museum and the discovery was noted in the Proceedings of the Somerset Archaeological and Natural History Society. This could so easily have been the end of the story but for the fact that 17-year-old Lionel Walrond, who lived in the neighbouring parish of Pitney, happened to read the reference to the tile's discovery in 1945. Lionel contacted Herbert Cook and together they dug another hole near to the grave of the sheep. More tile fragments were discovered. A local archaeologist was called in to help and a further excavation was carried out later in 1945. An area of mosaic was exposed. The pavement was fully uncovered the following year. It proved to be one of the most important Roman mosaics ever found in Britain. It is unique in telling a story, that of Aeneas and Dido taken from Virgil's *Aeneid* written in the 30s BC. The mosaic was lifted in 1953 and can be seen today in the Museum of Somerset.

Discovery of the Low Ham Roman mosaic

This is the tile found by Herbert Cook that led to the discovery of the Low Ham Roman mosaic.

View of the heating system in the bathing block of Low Ham Roman villa. Left and second left are Lionel Walrond and Herbert Cook whose actions led to the discovery of the Low Ham mosaic.

The Shepton Mallet amulet

In 1990 large-scale excavations took place alongside the Fosse Way at Shepton Mallet in advance of the building of a large warehouse for a drinks company. They revealed a previously unknown Roman town with roads, houses and workshops. There was also a cemetery of sixteen burials surrounded by a ditch. The grave of a man in the centre of the cemetery produced a silver amulet that lay close to his pelvis. The amulet was clearly a Christian object and caused much excitement. Christian objects from later Roman Britain are rare and none had ever been found in a grave. However, not all was what it seemed. The silver used to make the amulet was analysed. The results showed that the refining process used on the metal was sophisticated and could not have occurred before the nineteenth century. The amulet was a hoax! The construction of the new warehouse was very controversial. Although nobody has come forward to claim responsibility for planting the amulet, the suspicion is that it was one of a number of attempts to stop the development. It may have been hoped that the discovery of an object of national significance would be sufficient to prevent the building work going ahead.

The Shepton Mallet amulet with its Christian symbol proved to be a modern hoax.

Pyramid Stage, Glastonbury Festival

Somerset is known throughout the world for the Glastonbury Festival. The first Glastonbury Festival (called the Glastonbury Fayre) was held over two days at Worthy Farm, Pilton, in September 1970. Tickets cost £1 and included free milk from the farm. The 1,500 people attending saw acts including Marc Bolan, Al Stewart and Stackridge. The following year it was moved to the time of the summer solstice and admission was free. 1971 also saw the first incarnation of the iconic symbol of the Glastonbury Festival, the Pyramid Stage. It was constructed out of scaffolding and expanded metal covered with plastic sheeting. The performers that year included David Bowie, Joan Baez, Hawkwind, Traffic and Fairport Convention, major stars of the time, and 12,000 people attended. A permanent Pyramid Stage was built in 1981 made from telegraph poles and ex-MOD metal sheeting. The structure doubled up as a cowshed and animal food store during the winter months. This drawing shows the Festival in the 1980s when it was possible to camp near to the stage. This version of the Pyramid Stage burned down in 1994 shortly before the Festival was due to take place.

Since 1981 the Festival has been held more or less annually and grown to become a spectacular event attended by 135,000 people from around the world.

The Importance and Legacy of the Work of Victor Ambrus

By Kate Morton, Claire Thorne and Craig Williams, illustrators at the British Museum

Victor Ambrus is a master of his craft. An illustrator whose role in the *Time Team* team has given viewers, archaeologists and fellow illustrators the opportunity to see his drawings and paintings in the making. The superb quality of his illustrations has set the bar very high for others working in this niche field. Combining exceptional artistic flare with an academic integrity, the results are images that we know we can trust to be as good a visual reconstruction of a moment in the past as it is possible to have.

Victor's images are stunningly beautiful with a quality that is to be treasured for their intrinsic value and as an invaluable resource for future illustrators and archaeologists. They are packed full of lessons about how to research, how to look, how to collaborate and how to draw!

We know that the way we visualise the past is highly influenced by imagery in books and on displays in museums. This 'visualisation' of the past continues to be a hot topic in archaeological and historical research as computer-generated imagery is increasingly used to offer the viewer rich interpretations of past cultures, peoples, and the world they inhabited. Pencils allow a searching feel to a subject, with their less defined imagery and ability to add emphasis giving an ethereal tone as a subject enfolds. Victor reminds us that 'a picture tells a thousand words' and so those 'thousand words' worth of image-making must be well informed and carefully executed. Pencil drawings, he suggests, remain an ideal medium for illustrating past events because they are suggestive rather than emphatic; they say about the past, 'This is how it might have been.'

Archaeology offers clues about how people lived their lives but can offer nothing about their emotional existence. Victor's drawings explore, with such sensitivity, the impact of an event on human emotion. His images are therefore highly intimate and personal and we can relate to the people he has portrayed. An exhumed human skeleton cannot speak of emotional existence, but it can give clues to an individual's physical life experience and a possible cause of death. Victor's ability to put flesh on those bones, using his deep knowledge and understanding of human anatomy, reminds illustrators of the true value of life drawing. His sensitively drawn facial expressions (the result of a lifetime of observing and drawing the human face) create images full of character and personality. He can vividly describe the human condition whether in the terrifying moment of the kill or at a time of humour or farce. We are there, in the scene, and caught up in its energy. His drawings in this book bring the story of Somerset to life in ways never seen before. People, real and imagined, are at the fore, thereby bringing the county's history alive.

Victor's style is vivid and instantly recognisable. We can see how he uses a carefully chosen palette of colour for emphasis and energy. We can discover that his pictorial compositions, while full of detail, leave space for our imagination. They are landscapes full of natural life, which he has either drawn in situ or recalled from experience. They have spontaneity but are meticulously worked. They are evocative, dramatic, moody and atmospheric, they show us the value of closely observing the world around us.

Dig into a book of Victor's work – there is so much to see and learn.

Ambrus, V., and Aston, M., *Recreating the Past*, The History Press, 2001
Ambrus, V., *Drawing on Archaeology: Bringing History to Life*, Tempus, 2006
Ambrus, V., *Battlefield Panoramas: From the Siege of Troy to D-Day*, The History Press, 2012

ACKNOWLEDGEMENTS

Victor Ambrus, Steve Minnitt and the South West Heritage Trust express their grateful thanks to the following:

Lawrence Bostock, Keith Spicer and John Scaife for digitising the drawings, and Lawrence Bostock, Tina Bishop and Amal Khreisheh for helping to prepare them for publication; Pauline Rook and Justin Owen for permission to use their photographs featuring Victor Ambrus; Matilda Richards, Nicola Guy, Ele Craker and Zara Davis of The History Press for support throughout the creation of this book; Tom Mayberry for support and encouragement; Somerset Archaeological and Natural History Society for permission to use images in their collection; Sam Astill, Francesca Croft, Joy Minnitt, Esther Hoyle, Susie Simmons and Mary Siraut for their helpful comments on the text; Glenys Ambrus for her support and encouragement throughout this project.

Unless stated otherwise, photographs used are courtesy of the South West Heritage Trust. The museum objects illustrated in the book belong either to Somerset Archaeological and Natural History Society or Somerset County Council. Most are displayed in the Museum of Somerset, Taunton.

FURTHER READING

Aston, A. and Burrow, I., *The Archaeology of Somerset*, Somerset County Council, 1982

Aston, A. and Gerrard, C., *Interpreting the English Village: Landscape and Community at Shapwick, Somerset*, Windgather Press, 2013

Brunning, R., *The Lost Islands of Somerset*, Somerset Heritage Service, 2015

Brunning, R., *Avalon Marshes Archaeology: A Journey Into a Lost Landscape*, 2017

Coles, J., Minnitt, S. and Wilson, A., *Ceremony and Display: The South Cadbury Bronze Shield*, Somerset County Museums Service, 2000

Croft, R. (ed.), *Roman Mosaics in Somerset*, 2009

Dunning, R., *A History of Somerset*, Somerset County Council, 2003

Dunning, R., *The Monmouth Rebellion*, Dovecote Press, 1984

Hawkins, M., *Somerset at War*, Hawk Editions, 1995

Leach, P., *Roman Somerset*, Dovecote Press, 2001

Mayberry, T., *The Vale of Taunton Past*, Phillimore, 1998

Minnitt, S. and Coles, J., *The Lake Villages of Somerset*, Somerset Levels Project, 1996

Minnitt, S., *The Shapwick Treasure*, 2001

Moorhead, S., Booth, A. and Bland, R., *The Frome Hoard*, British Museum Press, 2010

Webster, C. and Mayberry, T., *The Archaeology of Somerset*, Somerset Books, 2007